Akemi's Journal
Volume 2

Akemi Tomoda

Akemi's Journal Volume 2 by Akemi Tomoda

Published by: Diamond Legacies

Diamond Legacies is an imprint of In Our Words, Inc. / inourwords.ca

Cover image and inside artwork: Akemi Tomoda

Library and Archives Canada Cataloguing in Publication

Tomoda, Akemi

[Diaries. Selections]

Akemi›s journals : testimony of the goodness of God in my life.

ISBN 978-1-926926-23-0 (v. 1 : softcover).--ISBN 978-1-926926-85-8 (v. 2 : softcover)

1. Tomoda, Akemi--Diaries. 2. Japanese Canadians--Diaries. 3. Christian biography--Canada. 4. Autobiographies. I. Title.

BR1725.T68A3 2012   248.8›43092   C2017-903800-1

All Rights Reserved. Copyright ©Akemi Tomoda, 2017. No part of this book may be reproduced in whole or in part, in any form, or stored on any device including digital media, except with the prior written permission of the author. Exceptions are granted for brief quotations utilized in critical articles or reviews with due credit given to the author.

Akemi's paintings of her backyard

Table of Contents

Introduction 1
In Gratitude 4
Welcome to the Lord's Garden 6
The Summer of 2010 9
Unwelcome Visitors in the Garden 12
Wonderful Surprises in 2010 16
I Slipped on the Ice 20
God's Invitation 24
The Summer of 2011 28
The Most Excellent Doctor 32
Visiting the Community Church 35
The Year 2011 40
Enter His Gates 43
"New Season for My Art Work" 46
The Kindness of God on Good Friday 50
From the Older Adult Centre 54
We Had a Guest Speaker 58
My Cataract Surgery 61
Precious Day in the Summer of 2012 65
My 75th Birthday 68
The New Fence 72
Christmas Gift from Our Heavenly Father 76
"Goodbye Eleanore" 80
The Celebration of My Books 83
Origami Cranes 87
I Received a Wonderful Ministry 91
I Needed Lots of Prayers 95
Restored Garden 98
From the Prayer Meeting 101
He Gave Me His Best 104
The Two Letters from Japan 108
The Year 2014 Started 111
A Visitor in the Cold Winter 115
Grocery Shopping with Marilyn 119
The Brand New Elevated Garden 123

Attacked by Bees..126
My Japanese Books were Published..................................129
Mirabilis in the Elevated Garden..132
The Gift of Painting 135
Precious Home Group 139
October Celebrations..142
The Healing Meeting at My Home.....................................145
The Unexpected Visitors 149
Precious Winter Break..152
Use My House for Your Glory 156
The Three Kind Men 159
The Month of Healing..164
Mike Published His Books 167
The Running Water...170
The Bird's Bath 173
The Dry Summer..176
Surrounded by Loving Sisters...179
Special Birthday Gift 183
I Had a Good Year in 2016 186
The Year 2017 Has Started 189
Thank You for Your Help 192

Introduction

I was born in a little village in Japan before World War II. My father was a school teacher, and his family believed in Buddhism for many generations, and my mother was a daughter of a Shinto priest. We experienced hardship and food shortage during World War II, but we managed quite well, and I was a happy child.

After I graduated from teacher's college I started to suffer from depression. At first it wasn't a big problem, but it became deeper and deeper and I did not want to live any more. I read so many books to find an answer to my problem, but I could not find any. During this time, I came across a tiny book *For the Sleepless Night* written by Carl Hilty. He wrote nothing but God's love and friendship with Jesus Christ which I did not understand at all. But one sentence from his book touched my heart deeply. He wrote "If you feel like shooting yourself in the head with a gun, read a Bible instead; and if you want to hang yourself with a rope, go to a church instead." I wanted to be free from depression so badly that I tried it. I started going to a church by riding a bicycle for 15 minutes and taking a train to the next city and walked about 30 minutes, because there wasn't a Christian church in our little village and there were no Christians. After a couple of years of struggle, I finally became a Christian in the year 1965. I was baptized in the name of the Father and the Son and the Holy Spirit at a little church in Mikara.

I met Ken Tomoda in the early spring of 1970 in Japan while he was on vacation from Canada to visit his family. We exchanged many letters and I decided to come to Canada to marry him in the fall of 1970, and lived in North York for several years and later moved to Mississauga.

In Canada, I experienced the Toronto Airport Church's revival, and I was touched by the Holy Spirit.

After several years of prayers, my husband became a Christian, and we read the Bible together and prayed together. We enjoyed beautiful times together. In January 2000, my husband invited Jesus into his heart, and his eyes started shining so beautifully. I was so happy to be with him, and only four months later one beautiful sunny Saturday morning he passed away suddenly from a massive heart attack.

That moment everything changed. I was overwhelmed by the grief of my husband's death and worries about my future living in a foreign country without a husband and children. I could not eat anything for two and a half weeks and shed tears every day for more than three months.

I just cried and cried, and one day I said to God with tears, "Lord, I can't live like this. My sorrow is so deep. I haven't touched the bottom of it. All our dreams were shattered and all our hopes were gone. I can't live like this." Then God spoke to me, "Akemi, my love is bigger than your sorrow, and deeper than your sorrow. My love is bigger than your shattered dreams and hopes." I thought about Jesus' death on the cross for me and for all human beings. Through my deep sorrow I came to know God's huge love for me.

It was very difficult, but I started living by myself one day at a time. It was very hard and I needed lots of help. I said to God, "Father I am in the fiery furnace. The fire is burning. Help me! If you fail to help me I can't survive."

God responded to my request. He helped me so wonderfully well by sending many kind people into my life. Many Christians helped me with prayers and encouragement, and many neighbours helped me in so many ways so that I was able to live without a husband and children.

God also helped me and healed me through writing essays. My English teacher, Eleanore Sproule visited me and taught me English even before my husband's death. After my husband's death, I could not think of anything, so I stopped taking English lessons, but I resumed it after a few months. Every time Eleanore visited me I presented one essay, and I decided to write about the goodness of God in my life. This helped me to go through the most difficult time in my life. I tried to see something good in my life instead of difficulties. I trained my mind to see something good. I also learned the importance of thanksgiving in my life, because God is bigger than any trouble I face on the earth.

God healed me with water colour painting. My husband loved art so much and he introduced me to art. He took me to New York, Chicago, Buffalo, Ottawa and Toronto to visit art galleries. After his death, I started taking art classes at Visual Arts Mississauga and found such joy in painting. When I paint, I lose myself completely in painting and nothing bothers me any more. I thank God for that.

God healed me through gardening. Ken left quite a big garden in my backyard. It was his garden and I did not touch it at all. But after his sudden death I had to look after the garden by myself. Right after I watered the garden for the first time I cried out to God, "Lord help me. I have to look after the garden by myself now. Send me someone who can help me to look after the garden."

Then two hours later, Phyllis, a lady who lived on our street, brought a young man to my home and said, "Akemi, this is Gary." I looked at the tall, handsome man who was silent. Phyllis said again. "Akemi, Gary wants to help you." Then Gary said, "I am your gardener." I cried. Since then, Gary has helped me in the garden and in the house too. He helped me a lot and I really thanked God for that.

In the year 2001, one Sunday in early summer I came home from church and opened the living room door to go out into the garden, and God spoke to me. "Thank you for looking after my garden." I was shocked and could not move for a long time. Since then I started calling my backyard "The Lord's Garden" and I started sensing the peace of God and enjoyed it so much. I also started seeing double rainbows in the garden every time I watered it. I was so excited to see the double rainbows and I thanked God.

Many years have passed since my husband's death. God has helped me and healed me so wonderfully well. He rescued me from the fiery furnace. He was with me all these years. I wasn't burned by the fire. I did not become angry or a bitter person. I am so thankful for that. I am still writing about the goodness of God in my life, and I thank God every time I write.

In Gratitude

By a miracle I became a Christian in Japan about 50 years ago. I just wanted to live my life without depression, but God took me into His family and poured out His love upon me.

My life wasn't an easy life. I went through many mountains and valleys, but God helped me to go through them wonderfully well. I am very thankful for that.

He sent me so many kind people to carry me through these difficult times.

I am grateful to Keith Sproule who offered to check my essays after my wonderful English teacher, Eleanore Sproule moved to Heaven. He called me and encouraged me to keep on writing my essays. I am very thankful for that.

I am thankful for my wonderful trustees, Janis Flower and Gary Brady. It's already 17 years since my husband Ken went to Heaven, yet they still look after me so well. Janis Flower calls me often and encourages me in spite of her busy life, and Gary Brady still visits me and cuts my grass so neatly, and helps me in so many ways. They make my life so safe. I really thank them.

I am thankful for Rita Gervais. She still visits me, and we pray together in my living room. Every time we pray together God joins us. What joy she has brought in my life! Thank you so much.

I am thankful to Anita Khan who is a beautiful sister in the Lord. She visits me often and helps me a lot. Her huge love for the Lord makes me so happy.

I am thankful for Elli Murach, our Bible study group leader, who demonstrates God's love and His kindness every time we meet. I have learned so much from her. I also thank God for Dianne Schleifer, Janette Schliephake, Freda K. Kayendeke, who bring a piece of Heaven to my life.

I am thankful for my sister, Sanae Sakurai, who lives in Japan. She calls me often and encourages me. She keeps on sending me Japanese goods to make my life easier.

The Lord has surrounded me with loving people and makes my life so peaceful. I am very thankful for that. He poured out His love, kindness and compassion over me. Sometimes I wonder why the creator of Heaven and earth loves me so much? But I learned that God loves every one of His children so deeply. From my very ordinary life I wrote these essays with a huge thanksgiving in my heart towards God.

Akemi

October 14, 2017

Welcome to the Lord's Garden

August 27, 2010

Since I started attending T.A.C.F. Mississauga in September 2009, I strongly felt that that was the church the Lord gave to me, and enjoyed attending there every Sunday. Within one year I took several courses, such as School of Champion I and II, Healing room training, Encounter weekend, and I came to know many people. I started feeling at home. I thanked God for this wonderful church every Sunday.

We have a program of "House blessing" in our church. When we request a house blessing, the church sends pastors or leaders to the house and pray over the house and the family. I wanted to invite Pastor Faustin and Marina Fernando for house blessing one day, but I wanted to invite them in summer time when the garden is in full bloom.

One day in winter when I talked to Pastor Faustin I said, "I really want to have you and your wife in my house, but it has to be in summer time. I have a beautiful garden in my backyard and I would like to show it to you."

"Of course, we will visit you Akemi."

That was a long time ago.

The garden season arrived this year again. I finished an art course in May, and English lessons in June, and became a gardener. I cleaned the garden, dug the soil, transplanted the perennials, watered, and enjoyed watching the garden grow. We had such warm weather in May that the perennials grew rapidly.

I was in the garden almost every day, and enjoyed the peace saturated in the garden. I started sensing the presence of the Lord many years ago, but it became stronger and stronger each year. This year I wanted to be in the garden as much as possible. I had breakfast in the garden, morning prayers and the Bible reading in the garden. I had lunch in the garden and sometimes I had supper in the garden.

In the beginning of July, the garden was in full bloom, and the time to invite Pastor Faustin and Marina arrived. On Sunday of July the 11th, I wrote on a piece of paper my request for a house blessing, my name, address, and telephone number, and gave it to Marina.

The following Sunday, on the 18th of July, Marina approached me before the service started and said. "Akemi, our family decided to go to California for a family vacation. We are leaving this week, so I would like to visit your home tomorrow. Is that okay with you?"

"Of course, it's okay with me. What time can you come?"

"I have to talk to my husband and I will let you know."

The date was set, but Marina did not have time to talk to her husband, so I did not know what time they were visiting me. I waited for a long time, but Marina was busy, so I came home. Marina called me from her house in the evening and told me that she and her husband would visit me at five o'clock on the following day.

On the 19th of July, I cleaned the garden neatly. The garden was filled with flowers. I also cleaned the house and prayed over the garden and the house. I asked God to bless our pastors' visit. I prepared iced tea and a bowl of summer fruits.

Faustin and Marina arrived around 5:30 pm. I invited them into the living room. When they sat on the sofa they looked at the flower garden through the glass doors. Faustin said. "It is so beautiful."

"Isn't it?" I said.

"It's so peaceful. I sense the presence of the Lord so strongly." Faustin wanted to thank God, and he choked up by the strong sense of His presence. We had a wonderful time in the living room, having a glass of iced tea and summer fruits.

"What do you do every day Akemi?" Faustin asked me. I pointed to my water colour painting on the wall of the living room and said, "I paint."

"Is that your painting?"

"Yes it is." I told them that I painted the memory of New York from the photo my husband took years ago. I also showed them *Akemi's Journal*, and told them that I still take English lessons from Mrs. Eleanore Sproule and write essays about the goodness of God in my life as my English homework. I also told them that I am a gardener in summer time. I told them how I lived and how much God helped me for the last ten years.

They wanted to go to the garden, so we walked into the garden. I told them about the gate which Gary made for me and named it the "Gate to Heaven." They enjoyed the flowers and the presence of the Lord in the garden.

"You should read the Bible in the garden," Marina said.

After walking in the garden, we came back to the living room and prayed for each other. I was so blessed by their powerful prayers. I showed them my water colour paintings hanging all over my house and they left with my recent essay "Thank you for the Last Ten Years."

I was so glad that I invited our pastors to my house. I truly enjoyed Pastor Faustin and his wife Marina's visit in the Lord's garden. I was so blessed by them, and hoped that they enjoyed the visit too. I said to God. "Thank you, Father. I had a wonderful time with Pastor Faustin and Marina. Thank you for your blessing over us." I just know that God enjoyed their visit to His garden too.

The Summer of 2010

September 23, 2010

The summer of 2010 officially ended on the 21st of September. It was a special summer I will never forget. It was unusually hot and humid through June and August. The temperature went up to the middle 30°C and with the humidity it was over 40°C. Some afternoons I would not even go out to the garden at all. I never experienced such humid weather since I came to Canada in 1970.

It reminded me of a Japanese summer. In Japan, right after the monsoon season, the hot and humid summer comes and stays for more than two months, July and August. I remembered that uncomfortable Japanese summer and was very unhappy. I said to God. "Lord I am living in Canada. Please give me Canadian summer weather." But this complaint did not work at all. The hot weather continued.

Later I talked to my sister Sanae in Japan and found out that this summer was unusually hot and humid in Japan too, and quite a number of deaths were reported from the heat. I realized that the weather of the whole globe was changing rapidly.

I had a very difficult time with this weather, but the plants in the garden grew healthily. The perennials bloomed gorgeously as usual. I watered the garden very early in the morning and watched the flowers from the living room.

We did not have our home group during summer time, but my friend Rita visited me some evenings, and we continued the smallest home group at my home watching the flowers.

One evening Rita mentioned that she did not have many days of work at the nursing home due to the change of management staff. I happened to have Arthur Burk's "Spiritual Warfare" CD discs from my friend Heather Caswell. I asked Rita if she wanted to listen to the discs some evening, and Rita agreed.

When Rita had time she visited me, and we listened to "Spiritual Warfare." It started on July 12th. We had a cup of tea and cookies or summer fruits, and started the evening with a short prayer. We listened to the CD watching the beautiful flowers in the garden. We truly enjoyed the strong sense of the presence of the Lord and His peace. We got together often as long as Rita and I were free, and finished listening to "Spiritual Warfare" on the 28th of July. When we finished "Spiritual Warfare" I was so glad and happy as if I accomplished some important thing.

Arthur Burk's teaching was very deep yet so clear. He portrayed the spiritual world so clearly from his personal experiences, that made me so interested.

I personally learned that I must discern the spirits and of course bind up and cast out the evil spirits. But I also learned the importance of the power of blessing. He emphasized that God's blessing is stronger than the enemies' curse. I had loved to pray blessing over people up to now, but since I heard this teaching I was determined to bless people more. I was so encouraged by his teaching. Rita and I finished listening to nine discs in hot and humid summer nights. It was so fulfilling, and I truly thanked God for the way we spent our time. I even wanted to celebrate our accomplishments in some way.

Then Rita said, "Akemi I have another Arthur Burk's teaching. It is called 'The Redemptive Gift.' Would you like to listen to this?"

"Sure. It would be nice."

"Okay. I will bring it tomorrow."

We started listening to another Arthur Burk's teaching on the 29th of July.

He taught us about seven redemptive gifts of prophet, servant, teacher, encourager, giver, leader, and mercy. We listened to one gift each evening.

This time Rita was called from the nursing home, so we had some breaks, but we continued to get together faithfully.

On the 23rd of August, I invited Rita to the sun room above the garage, and listened to the gift of teacher, and watched the two big orchid cactus blooming. When we started listening to the CD, the flowers had just started opening, but when we finished the CD, the flowers had opened completely. We watched two huge white fully bloomed orchid cactuses. It was a spectacular night. I marvelled at God's beautiful creation which still continues.

We listened to the "Mercy" on the 27th of August and finished the session. I learned so much from Arthur Burk's teaching. I learned these gifts are not only for special Christians but for everyone. God created each one of us in one of seven categories. That was truly an eye-opening experience for me. God did not create junk. He created each one of us so special, putting His DNA in us. I thought that we have to value ourselves more highly, because God created us.

Rita and I got together faithfully and listened to good teachings this summer. It took seven weeks. In these seven weeks, the flowers in the garden changed gradually. Some flowers finished and new ones started blooming. I thoroughly enjoyed the evening garden this summer.

I will remember the summer of 2010 as a hot and humid summer, but also as the summer I received good teaching. I thanked God for the way I spent this summer. I thanked Him for good teaching, a good friend, and most of all His presence every time Rita and I got together.

"Thank you, Father. It was a wonderful summer."

Unwelcome Visitors in the Garden

November 16, 2010

One day in early spring while I was driving on our street I saw a brown rabbit on the boulevard of Townwood Court. The rabbit was facing towards the end of the street, as if looking for a place to live.

But spring came. The air became warmer, and the sunlight became brighter, and each day daytime became longer. The flowers started blooming in the garden again. The pink tulips bloomed, and blue forget-me-nots followed. The bridal wreath at both sides of the hedge displayed a gorgeous sight as if the hedge were covered by white snow. I truly enjoyed the garden, and spent lots of time in it. Soon light mauve coloured wisteria flowers started hanging down from the trellis, and the purple and pink clematis bloomed proudly, and evening primrose added bright yellow colour in the garden. The garden was perfect as usual. I had breakfasts, morning prayers, and Bible reading in the garden and was satisfied.

Especially this spring a pair of cardinals and robins visited the garden often, drinking water from the bird's bath and picking food from the garden. Many squirrels were running around the garden as if it were their own garden. But it was quite a peaceful garden, and I was so pleased.

One summer evening while I was strolling in the garden I saw a dark object in a flowering bush and wondered what it was. When I approached, it had already disappeared.

A few days later my good friend Rita was with me in my living room listening to Arthur Burk's teaching. We watched the fully bloomed garden from the living room. Suddenly Rita said, "There is a baby rabbit in your garden."

"What?"

"Akemi. There is a baby rabbit. There," she pointed out and continued, "There are more. Three rabbits in the left side of your garden."

At the same time, I saw two rabbits running at the right side of the garden.

"There are two rabbits on this side. Oh no, there are five rabbits in the garden."

"What is the matter? Don't you like them? They are cute," Rita said.

"No, I don't like rabbits. They eat flowers."

I was shocked. There were five baby rabbits running all over the garden. I went out and chased them with a thin bamboo stick. They disappeared somewhere.

That big brown rabbit I saw on our street must have had five babies, and they were growing by eating plants all over our neighbourhood.

Every time I saw rabbits in the garden I chased them with a bamboo stick, but they came back soon again. I have the wire fence at both sides of my garden and the wooden fence at the back, but the bottom of the fence was wide open so that rabbits could come and go freely.

As long as I was in the garden I was able to scatter the rabbits, but I wasn't in the garden all the time. They ate the grass and left lots of droppings. I cried out to God. "Lord, rabbits are invading Your garden. They are eating the flowers in Your garden. Do something about it. I don't want to see the rabbits in Your garden." But God did not put an invisible net around the garden. The rabbits came again and again, and I chased them. They grew so fast. In a few weeks, they grew so big. They weren't babies any more.

One Sunday afternoon when I came home from church I found the false sunflower at the left side of the garden looking so much smaller. There had been at least 30 to 40 yellow flowers blooming, yet only five to six flowers were standing. I ran to the flowers and checked them. Many stems were cut off 15 cms above the ground, and the dead flowers were scattered on the ground. I picked them up one by one and took them to the yard waste bag. I felt so sad and upset. How could I chase the rabbits away? I did not know what to do. I could catch the rabbits in a trap, but I did not know what to do after that. "Oh God help me. Make Your garden free from the rabbits."

Eventually the false sunflowers were all gone, and the rabbits started eating the Echinacea's stems. I felt totally hopeless.

Then one night I had a dream about the rabbits. In my dream, the new spring came and the perennials started growing with new shoots, then the rabbits came and ate them all. There was absolutely nothing left. I woke up with perspiration all over my body. My heart sank. "Oh, Father is this the last year I enjoy the garden with You?" Maybe I have to change the garden from perennials to trees, like roses or hydrangeas. I felt so sad and cried out to God again. "God help me. Can't You do something about it."

One evening while Rita and I were in the living room and listening to Arthur Burk's teaching again the rabbits started hopping in the garden. Rita opened the glass door and went out to the garden and chased the rabbits away. When she came back she said, "Akemi put planks under the fence." I was shocked. What a simple idea, and yet I did not even think about that. Rabbits don't climb up like squirrels. What a wonderful idea! "I will. I will do it early tomorrow morning." I thanked Rita.

The next morning, I pulled out planks from the garage and put them under the fence, neatly holding them by bricks. Fortunately, Ken left lots of planks. I even took some out from the basement, and made a tight barricade all around the backyard.

Since I put the planks under the fence the rabbit invasion stopped. I did not see the rabbits in the garden for a few weeks. Then they started coming again, but this time only sometime, not all the time. I knew there was a gate for the rabbits to go through, but I could not find it.

Meanwhile the flower season came to an end, and I started

cleaning up the garden little by little. The day time was getting shorter and the air became cooler. When I had almost cleaned the garden suddenly the idea came to my mind to put a proper barricade under the fence. I thought about it and prayed about it often.

One weekend in November when Gary visited me, I asked him about putting a proper barricade under the fence. He said that he would do it for me. In the afternoon of November the 7th, Gary took me to Home Depot and obtained wire net and he placed it under the wooden fence so neatly digging the soil and stapling the net to the fence. He did a lot but the wire net ran out so he promised me he would do it the following day. Gary was so busy at his company, but he came to finish the barricade on the 13th of November. He did a good job. When he completed it I was so relieved. My worries and anxieties about the rabbit invasion were totally gone. I thanked Gary for his great help and also God that I have a rabbit-free garden again. He told me what to do through Rita and gave me a rabbit-free garden through Gary. I will enjoy the beautiful flower garden in the coming spring of 2011.

Roses from Rita

Jan 22, 2004

Wonderful Surprises in 2010

December 28, 2010

I celebrated Christmas and the year 2010 was coming to an end. It has been a very strange year. The winter was unusually mild and the summer was extremely hot. The weather pattern has changed quite a bit, but it wasn't only Canada, because the whole world experienced strange weather. I sensed that something had changed in the spiritual realm too.

I had a good year, and am very thankful to God. I sensed the presence of the Lord very strongly this year, and enjoyed doing everything with Him. I enjoyed attending our church very much. Our church Toronto Airport Christian Fellowship Mississauga changed its name to Catch the Fire Mississauga. I also enjoyed attending art classes, and enjoyed gardening in the summer season. I was in the garden almost every day, and strolled there and had a cup of tea sitting on a garden chair. The peace in the garden increased and I soaked in it.

This year has been a very special year, but I also experienced big surprises in the year.

The first surprise that I experienced was on the 21st of March. Our church had guest speakers from Stratford, Pastor Ivan and Isabel Allum. After the service, they prophesied over us. They picked some people and prophesied over them. I wasn't picked, but I got permission from our Pastor Marina and lined up and waited. I waited and waited. I waited until four o'clock.

Isabel came to me and started a tape recorder, and said. "Thank you Lord for the strong conqueror that you have been in difficult times and you are strong. You have been in a valley, and on a hill, and on a mountain. You have seen God's deliverance and His provision. You know God." She continued. "You are a strong intercessor and never stop praying. You are a friend of God, like Abraham and Enoch." Isabel explained to me that God will tell me what He is going to do, and I have to tell people God's will. I was shocked and thought that she was making a mistake or God was making a mistake. Anyway, she prophesied over me about seven minutes and told me that I was having a cup of tea with God. She quoted I Samuel 3:19 "The Lord was with Samuel as he grew up, and He let none of his words fall to the ground." She said to me. "God let none of your words fall to the ground."

I thanked Isabel, but I could not believe it was for me. I was utterly shocked. I was encouraged greatly but at the same time felt an enormous responsibility in my life. That was a big surprise.

The second surprise came to me on the Sunday of the 4th of July. I went to church 30 minutes earlier. I wanted to bless our church in my prayer. While I sat on a chair and prayed, Pastor Marina came and greeted me, and said, "Akemi come. Come with me. We are interceding for the church. Leave your bag here and come." I followed her and she led me to a hallway where three men and one lady were praying. Pastor Faustin, Bill Kelly, Feroze and his wife Anita were there. Marina and I joined, and soon the three men fell on the floor. When I prayed for Marina, she fell on the floor too.

After the service while I was going to leave the church, Pastor Faustin approached me and said. "Akemi. Please join our intercession prayer every Sunday. I want you to come one hour earlier."

"Thank you Pastor Faustin, but I am praying at the healing room on the second and fourth Sunday."

"Then come and join us the other Sundays. Okay?"

"Yes I will."

I started attending intercession prayers 1st and 3rd and 5th Sundays. Marina Fernando and June Bain were there. We three ladies prayed together. Marina is a pastor, and June was the organizer of the soaking room at Toronto Airport Christian Fellowship. She visited many countries on a mission trip. She is a big shot and I am nobody. I often asked God. "Lord. I am nobody. What are you doing to me?"

June visited me once at the end of the summer. We spent time with prayers and talking. I still go to the church one hour early to ask blessing over us. I enjoy it, but it was a big surprise to me.

I enjoyed attending our church very much, and also enjoyed art classes immensely. I met a wonderful teacher, Ann Fullerton, in 2006 when I took a drawing course at Visual Arts of Mississauga. Then I was still suffering from my husband's death, and for some reason Ann understood me. I also learned that she was teaching water colour painting too. I first took her water colour class in the fall of 2006. Since then I took Ann's water colour classes every year –10 weeks in spring and 10 weeks in fall. I enjoyed painting and also received so much healing in my life through painting. I was so happy to be at the class and to meet other artists.

I went to the class 30 minutes earlier than other people and arranged the tables for the class. The tables were quite long and heavy, but I learned the easy way to move the tables and arranged 15 tables and 30 stools.

On the last Tuesday of our course, the 23rd of November, while I was arranging the tables Ann came and thanked me.

"Akemi. Thank you so much for doing this every Tuesday."

"You're welcome Ann. I am so happy to be here. This is my gift for the class."

Then Ann said. "Akemi. What do you want to paint?"

"I would like to paint a street scene. Do you remember I painted the street scene of New York?"

"Yes I do. You did a good job."

"That picture is hanging in my living room. I love to paint street cars and people."

I also mentioned to Ann that I won't be able to attend the winter classes, because I don't feel comfortable driving in snow.

In the afternoon Ann said to the class.

"Class. We are going to paint flowers for four weeks and animals for four weeks in winter, and we are going to paint street scenes in the spring."

I was shocked, and thanked God in my heart for His favour over me.

Around three o'clock Ann came to me and said. "Do you have my telephone number Akemi?"

"No, I don't."

"I will give you my telephone number and address. Call me and visit me sometimes."

"Thank you so much." I gave my address and phone number to her.

"I am going to miss you Akemi."

"I will see you in the spring." I promised that I will paint as much as possible during the winter. It was a wonderful surprise to me.

I had many wonderful surprises this year. I would like to close the year with a big thanksgiving to God. But I realized that the most amazing thing is that God is with me all the time, as He promised.

"Never will I leave you

 never will I forsake you."

Hebrew 13:5

I embrace this incredible reality in my heart and close the year 2010 with a big thanksgiving to God.

I Slipped on the Ice

June 7, 2011

Early morning of March the 5th, I went outside to take my car out from the garage and slipped on the ice. It had started raining from the previous night and ice had formed on the driveway, but I did not know that. I picked myself up quickly and took the car out, and finished breakfast. I had pain in my right wrist, so I drove to a walk-in-clinic, in case something was wrong. When a lady doctor examined my wrist, it started swelling. She said to me, "You have to go to the emergency immediately." She gave me a paper. When I drove home I could not use my right hand at all.

I called Gary and asked him to take me to the emergency. He came soon and drove me to the emergency of the Credit Valley Hospital. At the hospital I was sent to take an x-ray, and a young doctor examined me and put on a temporary cast. He told me to see a specialist at the hospital next Monday.

Gary drove me home. Suddenly I was in panic realizing that I had to live by using my left hand alone for the next few weeks. I asked Gary to remove my wrist watch and rings. I knew it would be a very challenging time ahead.

Next Monday, March the 7th, my good friend Rita took me to the hospital. I went to the Fracture Department. I registered and waited to see a specialist. While I was waiting I saw so many people who had fractured their bones. Some were sitting on the chairs and there was a long line up to register. I thought it was just like a fracture factory. I was amazed that so many people broke their bones. I talked to a lady who was sitting next to me. She seemed to have difficulty with her leg.

"Did you break your leg?"

"Oh no, I broke my hip bone. I wish I broke my leg."

"I am so sorry. I hope you will be healed soon."

I truly thought that my case was a very minor case.

My name was called and Dr. Macguy examined me. He told a young technician to put on a proper cast and told me to come and see him in five weeks.

Rita drove me home. On the way she took me to Longo's to do grocery shopping and took me home. She carried all my groceries into the kitchen and cut all the vegetables for me, and opened the bottle of fruit drink. I was so touched by her kindness.

I thought my case was a very minor one and would be alright soon, but I found out that it was very challenging to live with using my left hand alone. Everything took so much time and effort. When I woke up in the morning it took a very long time to make my bed and change my clothes. Wearing pantyhose and a bra using my left hand was very challenging. When I finished breakfast, I wanted to have a nap.

After only a few days after my injury, on the 11th of March, huge earthquakes hit Japan, and gigantic tsunamis destroyed Japan so badly. I became so busy with praying for Japan. On Sunday of March the 17th, Pastor Faustin invited me to the front and asked me to pray for Japan. Rita took me to Yan Wah's prayer meeting and also Meadowvale prayer group to pray for Japan with other Christians. I truly desired that Japanese people would come to know their own creator, the loving God. I sincerely asked God to send the big tsunamis of salvation to Japan, and Japanese people would find the love of God in their lives. While I was busy with praying for Japan the time went very quickly.

The Lord sent me wonderful helpers again and again in my life and carried me through so wonderfully. Rita took me to grocery stores often and cut vegetables for me. Pastor Faustin visited me with a young man, Storm, with two bags of groceries and prayed over me. He also picked me up early Sunday mornings. He is quite busy on Sunday morning yet he took time for me. One Sunday he was at Hamilton and Anita Khan came to pick me up with another grocery bag. I was deeply moved by the love of the brothers and sisters in the church.

One day a big snow storm hit, and I found my neighbour Pat was cleaning my driveway. I went out and thanked her. When she saw the cast on my right hand she said. "Don't worry. I will clean your driveway for you."

I thanked her from the bottom of my heart. We had a very cold and snowy March, and Pat helped me again and again.

One day Theresa who lives across the street asked me if I needed anything. I forgot to buy a bottle of fabric softener so I asked her to get fabric softener. Then next morning her mother Nora brought me a bottle of fabric softener and a package of frozen lasagna. When I asked her "How much do I owe you?" She said. "No, no. These are gifts for you. Get well soon Akemi." I was so touched by the people who live on our street.

One day Christine who used to live on our street visited me and vacuumed the staircases for me and delivered a cooked meal the following day.

Carol Hay invited me for dinner one evening and offered me a big spoon so that I was able to eat delicious food easily with my left hand.

Diego, who cuts my wisteria every fall, called me and asked me if I needed anything.

In five weeks God sent me so many wonderful friends to help me. I was so thankful for that.

After five weeks, on the 11th of April, Janis took me to the hospital and Dr. Macguy checked the result of the x-ray and said "Your bone is healed. We will remove your cast today. You go to physio and come to see me in five weeks." My cast was removed. Janis took me home and I was so relieved. I was able to use both hands now. I was able to drive the car, and wash my face with both hands. I was so happy.

After seven visits to physio my right wrist healed wonderfully. I still had pain so it took a long time to write, but eventually I was able to write letters.

It was a very painful experience but I received so much help and love from my friends and neighbours. I thanked God for His wonderful care through wonderful people.

Painting of Gary

God's Invitation

July 18, 2011

My good friend Rita invited me to attend Young Wah's prayer meeting at the end of the year 2010. I knew she was attending that meeting for many years faithfully, I never wanted to go there. I don't like to attend many meetings, especially at night. I rather like to have a quiet and peaceful night at home. That satisfies me.

But when Rita said, "Would you like to go to Young Wah's prayer meeting with me? It is held the first Monday of the month."

I sensed that the Lord was inviting me to the prayer meeting. I was quiet for a moment, and thought in my mind that I had to consider it seriously, because God was so good to me and helped me so much. Now it was time to return to God everything He restored to me. I said, "Rita, I really like to stay home at night, but I think I have to attend the prayer meeting. Please take me."

"Oh good! The next one will be January the third. I will pick you up around 6:30. Okay?"

"Thanks."

On the third of January, Rita took me to Young Wah's residence in the south of Mississauga. It looked to me to be quite a long drive. When we arrived at Young Wah's big, beautiful house there were already many people in the kitchen. Young Wah welcomed me so warmly and made me very comfortable.

I was invited to the big room in the basement. There were a few people sitting on the chairs and on the floor. There was a fireplace at the right side of the wall. There was a sofa, several wooden chairs, and many big oriental cushions on the floor. When I sat on the sofa with Rita I faced a huge world map painted on the entire wall. There were many pins on the map. There was a paper world map, a Bible, lots of printed papers and a horn placed on the floor. I thought that they were doing God's business seriously.

The meeting started. Young Wah introduced me to the other people and asked me to tell how I became a Christian. She said. "There are not many Christians in Japan. How did you become a Christian? Tell us about your testimony."

I gave a very short version of my testimony, and thanked God deep in my heart for my miraculous salvation.

We heard reports from Young Wah and responded to the reports by prayers. At the end, each one of us prayed for our own country in our own language. People came from so many different countries, Korea, Iran, Iraq, Egypt, Italy, Canada, and Japan. I prayed in Japanese for the salvation of Japanese people. I was so glad that I went there.

I came home and thanked God for His invitation to that meeting, and I was able to pray for Japan.

I missed the next meeting because of my backache. I broke my right wrist on the 5th of March and missed the March meeting. The big earthquake and tsunamis hit Japan. I kept on praying for Japan by myself.

When I attended the meeting on the 4th of April, I was still wearing a cast on my right arm. People welcomed me and prayed for healing over me.

> One lady gave me Psalm 93 for Japan.
> *The Lord reigns, He is robed in majesty;*
> the Lord is robed in majesty
> and is armed with strength.
> The world is firmly established;
> it cannot be moved.
> Your throne was established long ago;
> you are from all eternity.
> The seas have lifted up, O Lord,
> the seas have lifted up their voices;
> the seas have lifted up their pounding waves.
> Mightier than the thunders of the great waters,

Mightier than the breakers of the sea –
the Lord on high is mighty.
Your statutes stand firm;
Holiness adorns your house
for endless days, O Lord.

As usual everyone prayed for his or her country in his or her own language. I prayed for Japan that the Lord would reign over Japan and that salvation like a tsunami will wash over Japan again and again. I was so glad I went there and was able to pray for Japan. I truly thanked God for that.

On the 11th of July, Rita and I went to the meeting. That evening there were so many people gathered at Young Wah's house. Five missionaries joined us. One couple came from South Korea, one couple came from Senegal, and a lady from Thailand. We introduced ourselves briefly and prayed for the nations. It was an awesome meeting. I sensed the presence of the Lord strongly and felt joy in my heart.

Each one prayed for his or her own country in his or her own language again putting our hands over our country on the map on the wall.

I prayed for Japan putting both my hands over Japan on the wall. People joined me in tongues and put their hands over my back. I said again and again. "Lord this land is your land. These people are yours. Come and reign over us. Save us."

When I finished praying and came back to the sofa, a young missionary, Jason, came to me and said.

"Could you give me a hug?"

"A hug?" I asked.

"Yes, a hug. Could you give me one?"

"Of course."

I hugged him and blessed him. Then he said. "When you were praying for Japan I saw a picture of Jesus. He was holding Japan in

His hands. I believe something will happen in Japan.

"Yes, I believe so."

I came home with a big thanksgiving in my heart towards God. I only attended Young Wah's prayer meeting four times, yet I felt so comfortable and at home. I looked forward to the next meeting. I was so sure that God invited me to these prayer meetings. I am so grateful that God can use even my prayers.

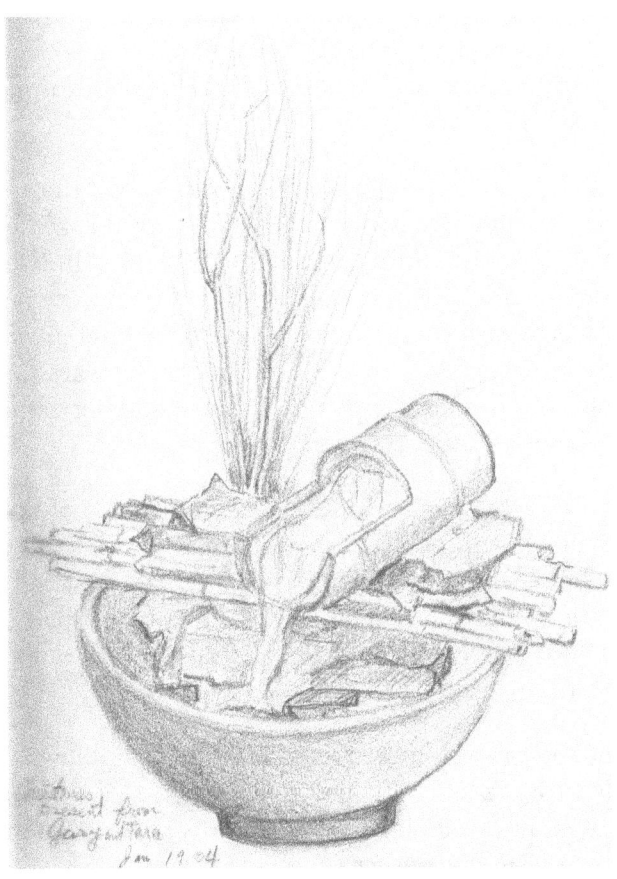

Christmas present from Gary and Tara

Jan 19, 2004

The Summer of 2011

August 25, 2011

The summer of 2011 started with a big expectation for the garden. Because the garden was damaged badly by many rabbits last summer, I asked my dear friend Gary to close the bottom of the wooden fence with wire net, and put planks under both sides of the wire fence. He did a good job. I felt so good knowing the garden was rabbit free and secure. I expected to have a beautiful garden this summer.

One day in early summer, I saw a baby rabbit running in the garden and was shocked. I could not believe what I saw. How did it come into my garden? Did it come through the tiny hole in the wire fence? I could not figure out how it had come into the garden, but the rabbit was there. I found there were two baby rabbits in the garden eating many soft stems of the perennials. They are fussy eaters, and eat only certain kinds of plants. They caused big damage in the garden.

I went to Terra Nursery and obtained a bottle of spray and a box of perrets, but none of them worked. It was so sad to see the perennials being eaten by the rabbits every day. I prayed hard and in the middle of the summer the rabbits finally stopped coming to my garden. But the damage was already done. I did not see several flowers bloom this year.

The hot and dry summer arrived. We had only a few rain days in July. The land was extremely dry. The temperature went up to over 35°C, and with humidity it was close to 50°C. These hot and humid days continued for a few weeks.

I watered the garden at six o'clock each morning and could not go out during the day. The flowers bloomed, but did not last long under the scorching sun. I was so disappointed and sad. I never experienced a miserable garden like this.

The garden wasn't so beautiful this summer, but the peace of the Lord was still there, and every time I watered – of course the sun must be on my back – the double rainbows appeared in the air. That thrilled me. Every time I saw the double rainbows in the garden I said to the Lord "Thank you Lord. You still give me the double rainbows. As long as I feel Your presence in the garden and see the double rainbows I am very happy. It is Your garden. The rainbows are Your signature. Thank you."

This summer was a very unusual one. One day in early summer my sister, Sanae, called me from Japan, and informed me that our mother was dying. She had lost her memory and stopped eating completely. The doctor told Sanae that he wouldn't put a tube into her stomach, because she is already 98 years old. The doctor mentioned that it takes two to three weeks to die, so be prepared.

Sanae said. "You don't have to come back here. It's too far and we can handle it."

"Thank you," I said.

"I already called the funeral home and told them about my mother. Then a lady said that as soon as mother dies they will pick up her body and cremate it. I asked her for a small room for a funeral because it's going to be a very small funeral. The lady said everything will be taken care of. So everything is okay."

"Thank you so much for what you are doing. I really appreciate it. Please let me know when she dies."

"Of course I will."

My mother is not a Christian. I prayed for her salvation every day for more than 35 years, but nothing happened. I was so sad to see my mother dying without knowing her Saviour.

One evening my friend Rita visited me, and we prayed as usual. While we were praying I wanted to pray for my mother. I asked for forgiveness on behalf of her that she had lived her whole life without acknowledging her Saviour. It could have been a beautiful life with His blessings. I addressed her spirit and introduced the Lord Jesus.

I prayed. "Lord Jesus this is my mother. Mother this is your creator. You do not know, but He created you." I asked God to take her into heaven because she is my mother.

I waited for my sister's call for three weeks, but she did not call me. I waited another week, but I did not hear from her at all. After five weeks, I called Sanae and asked about our mother.

"Oh, I sent you a letter weeks ago."

"We are having a mail strike now. I don't receive any letters now-a-days. How is mother?"

"Oh, she is okay."

"What?"

"Her memory came back, and she can eat now."

"Really?" I was shocked.

My sister told me that she was visiting mother at the nursing home three times a week. But she was too exhausted to visit for a few times. So she skipped. The next time she visited mother she could not find her in her room. She thought that somebody had stolen mother's body. She looked for mother all over frantically and found her in the cafeteria eating food. Sanae told me that one of the caretakers said to her, "Your mother is resurrected."

After I talked to my sister I was so thrilled at what the Lord did for my mother. I truly believed that He touched her body and also her spirit too. I thanked God for that.

Recently Sanae called me and said. "Can you make smocks for mother? Cardigans are not easy to wash. If you can make some smocks for her they're very easy to wash."

"Of course I can. How many smocks do you need?"

"About four."

"Four of them? Wow! I will."

I decided to buy material the next week and start making them before my art class starts.

After all, the summer of 2011 wasn't bad at all because the Lord was with me. I am so thankful for that.

In August, the heat wave was gone and the weather became very comfortable. I started enjoying being in the garden planning for a beautiful garden for the year 2012.

Simone's flower ring ~ sketch and finished watercolour

Jan 23, 2004

The Most Excellent Doctor

October 10, 2011

I have suffered from neck pain and back pain for about 35 years. The pain was only on the right side, and sometimes it came to my right eye and right elbow. I had seen doctors twice concerning my neck pain. The first one was 30 years ago and the second one was about 20 years ago. Both times the doctors sent me for physio, but it really did not work. The pain came back again. I realized that doctors could not do anything about it, and I had to live with the pain.

I tried everything to reduce pain, like painkillers, ointment, massage, etc. Fortunately, the pain left me sometimes but unfortunately it came back again. That was my life. I just had to live with it.

Two years ago, I started attending a new church in Meadowvale, Toronto Airport Christian Fellowship Mississauga Campus, and received training about God's healing. At that time, I had big hopes about losing my pain, and started saying "I am healed" repeatedly. At the same time, I found out that my right leg was half an inch shorter than my left one. I made a cushion about a quarter inch thick and put it in my right shoe. Then I started feeling much better with my neck pain, and gradually the pain left me.

Since then, I had one-and-a-half years of pain-free life. It was so wonderful and I thanked God every day.

But one day the pain came back as if it was there all the time. I tried everything to get rid of it, but could not succeed. I was in pain again. I really needed to see a doctor.

The middle of July my family doctor moved to Lakeshore and Mississauga Road. Once I drove there to find out how to get to the new building. But it was way too far. I thought I needed a new doctor closer to me, because when I need a doctor I am sick and cannot handle a long-distance drive. Even if I call a cab it would be so expensive.

I started looking for a new doctor, and soon found out that not many doctors take new patients now-a-days. I asked many of my friends to ask their doctors to take me as a new patient, but it did not work. I visited many doctor's offices but no doctor accepted new patients. Finally, I found one doctor who took new patients very close to my home. I was so thankful for that, and thanked God that I did not have to drive so far. Dr. Surangiwala is my new doctor.

One day I visited my new doctor and decided to talk about my neck pain. While I was in a little exam room I asked God to heal me and said "Lord please help me. I know doctors could not do anything about my neck pain before. But I need your help. You spoke through a donkey. You can speak through a non-Christian doctor. Help me."

When Dr. Surangiwala came to the room I explained about my neck pain and that I did not have pain last year after I raised my shoe. But it came back again and it was so painful. Dr. Surangiwala listened to me patiently to my surprise. She said. "Raise the cushion. It must be worn out after a year." I said in my heart, "Thank you Lord. You spoke to me."

The doctor arranged to take an x-ray and I went to the x-ray clinic soon. Then I went to Shoppers Drug Mart to buy a pair of insoles. I came home and constructed a new cushion a little higher than the last one.

The pain was still there, but I tried to be positive and joyful. I tried to think about the goodness of God alone in my life. One morning I drove to the community centre and walked around the Lake Aquitaine. I decided to thank God every step and succeeded. I thanked God for many things and felt good even though I still had pain.

A few days later, the first Sunday in October we had a pot luck lunch at the church. While I was eating lunch Mike Whate, the leader of our healing room joined me. While we were eating lunch, I mentioned about my neck pain and also my short right leg. Then he put his plate on the next chair and said. "Let me pray over your leg."

"Now?"

"Yes. Stretch out both legs." He held both my legs with both his hands and said. "Yes, your right leg is shorter than the left one. Father, stretch Akemi's right leg." He kept on praying and said.

"It's coming. It's coming."

"What?" I could not believe it.

"Look your legs are same now."

I truly could not believe it, but my right leg was stretched about half an inch.

A couple of days later when I visited the chiropractor I asked him to weigh both my legs. They have special scales to weigh both legs separately. Dr. Dugun agreed and checked my legs and found out that my legs were even.

I came home and removed the cushion from my shoe, and bought new slippers, because the old ones had a quarter inch added on the heel.

I truly thanked God for what He did to me and felt so safe to have Dr. Jesus as my doctor. My neck and back pain are going gradually. I know it will go completely. I thank God for that too. Praise the Lord!

Diane's chrysanthemum

March 18, 2004

Visiting the Community Church

December 2, 2011

On the 2nd of November right after I had breakfast I went out and trimmed the yew tree in the front yard. It grew so high and bushy. I cut a big branch with a saw and trimmed many branches with a pair of garden scissors. It was a beautiful autumn day, and I enjoyed working in the yard. It took more time than I expected, but I trimmed the tree nicely, and picked up all the branches from the ground and put them into a yard waste bag. I felt so good at what I accomplished.

As soon as I got into the house the telephone rang.

"Hello."

"Is this Akemi?"

"Yes."

"This is Anne. Anne Span. Do you remember me?"

"Yes I do. How are you?"

"I am not good Akemi. I have been sick for a while. I have bacteria in my body and suffered a lot."

"I am so sorry."

"I got your telephone number from Marlene Traas. I would like to see you."

"Please come and visit me. As a matter of fact we have a healing room in our church on Friday evenings. Would you like to come?"

"No, I don't think so. I am too tired to do that."

I prayed over her for healing over the phone.

"Thank you, Akemi. Can you come and see us at the Community church in Meadowvale on the 20th of this month? We are going there."

"At the Community church? I think I can. I will see you there."

I was surprised to hear from Anne Span. It was about six or seven years ago that one summer evening about a dozen intercessors got together and prayed over a young missionary couple – John and Anne Span. They were back from Guinea to Canada for a short time.

When I arrived at the church and went to the big room in the basement John approached me, and we introduced ourselves. Then suddenly John said to me. "There are lots of persecutions there. We are having a very hard time."

"I understand very well," I said. "I became a Christian in Japan, and my mother was very upset about it. It's not easy to be a Christian."

Soon Pastor Sam came and prayer started. Then John said, "I want Akemi to pray over me."

I was shocked, but what could I do? I moved next to John, and Pastor Sam came and put his hand over my back. I don't recall anything I prayed, but one thing I still remember clearly was that while I was praying suddenly I sensed God's thought to John. I said. "John, I sense that God is saying to you 'Thank you for giving me your life. I cherish it and honour it.'"

Then John burst into tears. He cried so loudly. He cried almost the whole night. We, intercessors, all prayed over him and his wife Anne. Pastor Sam washed their feet.

That was many years ago. Last year Marlene Traas told me that John Span was ordained to be a pastor. Marlene did not attend the ceremony, but she heard from her friend that when John became a pastor he gave a speech, and he said that years ago he and his wife went to the Community church in Meadowvale and a lady called Akemi prayed over them. Since then they have been changed completely.

When I heard that I was truly shocked. Of course, God can use anybody. He can speak through anybody. He can even speak through a donkey. I happened to be there and God used me. But still it was an honour to be used by God. I truly thanked Him for that.

On the 18th of November, I visited the Community church. I met Pastor Sam and the secretary Nan, at the pastor's office. I confirmed John and Anne Span's visit to the church on the 20th, when it was time to start the service. I told them that Anne Span called me and wanted to see me. I was glad for what I did.

On Sunday, November the 20th, I drove to the Community church at 9:30 am. It was a little too early, but I was able to park my car easily. There were already four or five cars in the parking lot. I shut off the engine of the car and relaxed. I decided to stay in the car a little while. I leaned my head back on the car seat and closed my eyes. I felt such peace and praised God in my heart. "Lord thank you. You are so good. The life with you is so exciting."

When I opened my eyes, I saw a lady approaching my car. She was smiling at me, and I realized that it was Anne. I got out of the car and greeted her. "Good to see you Anne."

"Thank you for coming Akemi. May I sit in your car?"

"Of course."

We sat in my car and talked. I prayed for her healing again. Anne shed tears. I reached for a box of facial tissues from the back seat and gave it to her. I got out of the car and opened the trunk and took out my bag and a gift of a new calendar. While I was taking out my bag a few cars started arriving in the parking lot. A young man came out from a van and ran to me. Daniel came and gave me a tight hug.

"Good to see you Daniel. How are you?"

"I am good."

"Daniel, I am talking to Anne Span in my car. I will see you in the church okay? Can you wait for me?"

"Sure," he said.

I sat in the car again and read Luke 10:18-19.

He replied, "I saw Satan fall like lightning from Heaven. I have given you authority to trample on snakes and scorpions and overcome all the power of the enemy; nothing will harm you." I said, "Jesus is telling you Anne, when you do His job nothing will harm you. I want you to receive this word from the Lord. He can't lie. This is the truth."

"I will meditate on it," Anne said.

I said to her, "Anne, I challenge you. Which do you spend more time on, worrying about your sickness or praising and thanking God?"

"I think I spend more time worrying about sickness."

"Could you switch that? Think about God's goodness and thank Him more. That changes the atmosphere. Could you please try it?"

"I will. Definitely I will do that."

I gave her a new calendar of my garden and explained it to her. I showed her the double rainbows in the month of August, and told her that God blesses my garden. Anne thanked me, and we walked into the church.

In the lobby Daniel was waiting for me. Daniel and I sat together as we used to do years ago. While I was attending the Community church Daniel was always with me, and we made origami – Japanese paper craft together. That time he was small, but now he is much taller than I am. We sang hymns together and listened to the sermon which John Span delivered. I asked Daniel, "Do you still remember origami?"

"Yes, I remember everything I did."

Daniel loves art. I took both his hands and prayed over him. "Father increase your gift of creativity over him, increase your gift of sensitivity towards beauty."

When the service ended Daniel left. We promised to see each

other in the Christmas holidays.

Right after the service one of the elders came to me and shouted, "Akemi, is that you? Good to see you! Can you join us to pray for Anne? We are going to pray for her."

"I will. Thank you for inviting me."

Soon Pastor Sam came and said, "Akemi, could you pray for Anne?"

"Yes, I can. Cynthia already invited me."

"Good."

About seven people surrounded Anne and prayed over her. I felt the spirit so strongly. Anne was very pleased. I talked to John and blessed him. I said good-bye to Anne with a warm hug. Anne said, "Thank you for coming. I would like to visit your garden one day."

"Yes. Please do next summer."

I was so glad that I went to the Community church on the 20th of November. It was quite a mild beautiful autumn day. I drove home happily with a deep thanksgiving in my heart for the Lord.

The Year 2011

December 9, 2011

The year 2011 started peacefully. I enjoyed the quiet winter with white snow. Then one day in early March I slipped on the icy driveway and broke my right wrist. I had excruciating pain so that I could not sleep for a couple of nights. I could not drive or cook. I could not even wash my face properly. I suffered so much from the pain and inconvenience. I said to myself, "My God is bigger than my problem." Then God spoke to me. "Be of good cheer. I am with you. I am in you."

God sent me wonderful helpers and met all my needs miraculously. My good friend Rita took me to the grocery shops many times, cut vegetables, and opened cans. For five weeks, Pastor Faustin Fernando picked me up on Sunday mornings and drove me to church and my friend Ellie drove me home. I recovered wonderfully well.

Then Japan was hit by earthquakes and tsunamis. The country suffered great destruction and 21,000 people died. I increased prayers for the salvation of the Japanese people. I have been praying for Japanese people's salvation for many years, but nothing had happened there. In Japan's neighbouring countries, like Korea and China, people were receiving Jesus rapidly, but not in Japan. I started thinking that no matter how much I pray nothing will happen because the enemies are too strong. Then I said to myself. "My God is bigger than the enemies. He will take Japanese people and Japanese land. One day every knee will bow down and every tongue will proclaim Jesus as the Lord." Then God spoke to me, "Be of good cheer. I am with you. I am in you." I pray for Japan by myself and with a group believing that God will bring the waves of salvation to Japan.

One day in spring my English teacher Eleanore Sproule's husband Keith Sproule called me and told me that Eleanore couldn't drive a car any more. Eleanore had been my English teacher for more than eleven years. She helped me so much not only in teaching me English, but also healing my life. Especially when I lost my husband she helped me tremendously. I received so much healing by writing essays about my husband's death and sorrow. Every time she visited me I presented one essay. I truly enjoyed having her in my home. I felt so sad and said to myself, "My God is bigger than this problem." God said to me, "Don't be discouraged. I am with you. I am in you."

Later Eleanore found out that she has Lou Gehrig's Disease. But I decided to continue writing my essays about the goodness of God in my life, and sent them to Eleanore. She checked my essays and sent them back to me. I am so thankful for that.

One day in October my friend Rita and I visited Eleanore. I had a good time with her. Rita and I prayed over her. That was such a blessing to me. I keep on praying for her healing.

In the summer two baby rabbits invaded my garden and ate lots of stems of the perennials. That upset me so much. I tried everything to prevent them from coming in, but nothing worked. They came through the tiny holes of the wire fence. I could not even plant new plants this year. The garden was damaged badly, and I felt so hopeless. I was afraid to go out and find more damage done by the rabbits. After many prayers I said to myself, "God is bigger than this problem." And God said to me, "Be of good cheer. I am with you. I am in you."

Eventually the rabbits stopped coming. In the fall, I asked my friend Diego to fix my garden and he put chicken wire all around the garden. It was a very difficult job but he did it wonderfully well. I was so pleased. I can see the garden with a peaceful mind and had big expectations for the coming spring again.

At the end of July my family doctor moved to the Lakeshore and Mississauga Road. It was quite a distance to drive from my house. I was so anxious about that. I knew he was moving from last year, but could not find a doctor who takes new patients. I asked my friends and visited many doctor's offices, but none of them took new patients. I said to myself, "My God is bigger than my problem. He will give me a new doctor." Then He said, "I am with you. I am in you.

Be of good cheer."

Finally, I found one doctor very close to my house, and I was so pleased. I have seen her many times already, and she helped me so much. I am very thankful for that.

My sister Sanae called me from Japan this summer and told me that our mother was unconscious and stopped eating food completely. The doctor told Sanae that mother would die in two to three weeks. Sanae was preparing a funeral. I really worried about this situation because mother was dying without knowing Jesus. I introduced Jesus to my mother's spirit in my prayer. Then she recovered miraculously. In a couple of months later she was hospitalized from heavy bleeding. After she recovered from the bleeding Sanae called me and asked me for a prayer. She said, "Mom is getting better, and the hospital doesn't want to keep her any longer. The nursing home does not want to have her back because Mom needs a special diet. Please pray. I really don't know what to do." I asked the Lord to open the door of the nursing home miraculously. Then I said to Him. "No Lord. I don't have to tell You what to do or how to do it. You know the best. Give my mother Your best." I said to myself. "My God is bigger than this problem." Then He said to me. "I am with you. I am in you. Be of good cheer."

Soon my mother died on the 10th of September at the age of 98. My sister called me and said. "I never thought of this, but this is the best for her and for us. Mom looked so peaceful when she died. I am so glad." It is so strange but I started feeling so close to her.

The year 2011 has been a very stormy year for me. I faced so many difficulties and problems, but God helped me to go through all the difficulties and problems. I decorated the living room with a Christmas tree and Christmas lights to celebrate the birth of Jesus. I truly enjoyed "Immanuel," God is with us, this year. I am expecting a wonderful and exciting year 2012, knowing that God goes with me, like He often said to me, "I am with you. I am in you. Be of good cheer."

Enter His Gates

January 30, 2012

One Sunday morning Pastor Faustin asked me. "Akemi, would you like to be a cell leader?"

"No, I don't," I answered.

"Then can you have one lady. She is looking for a place to go." Pastor Faustin explained to me that Anita Khan was looking for a cell group to attend. Anita and her husband Feroze have their own home group, and they attended at Pastor Faustin's cell group at night when cell leaders got together. But Anita could not attend that meeting any more, because of her children, and is looking for a new group to attend during the day.

"Could I send her to you?"

"What do I do?"

"Just spend time with her."

I thought that I could spend time with her. It's not difficult.

"Okay, I can do that. Just spend time with her right?"

"Yes, that's all. Thank you. I will tell her."

After the service Anita talked to me personally and confirmed that she would come and spend time with me. That was in early summer of 2011.

On Wednesday of June the 15th, Anita visited me for the first time. I prepared for the meeting by cleaning the house and the garden, and with lots of prayers. After my prayers, I sensed that we should build ourselves up in Christ to become overcomers. I agreed with God.

Anita arrived around 10:30 am, and we sat on the garden chairs in the garden. We talked, read the Bible and prayed surrounded by the flowers. It was really a relaxed atmosphere and I enjoyed it very much. I realized that God looked after our meeting and enjoyed being with us. I truly thanked Him. Anita left a little after 12 pm.

Anita visited me every other Wednesday through the summer. Every time we got together, we thanked God and praised Him. We talked, read the Bible, prayed and blessed each other. It wasn't difficult. I enjoyed the presence of the Lord and Anita's visit.

One day the Lord impressed on me to increase thanksgiving and praise to Him. So I mentioned it to Anita and we really thanked God for everything we could think about and praised Him from the bottom of our hearts. I thought that Anita might be tired of thanking and praising God every time we met, but she visited me continually, and we kept on thanking God and praising Him. The colours of the garden changed every week, and the summer went gradually. Anita and I developed a beautiful friendship, and I enjoyed being with her. She is a genuine sweet lady.

One day in September Anita invited me to a BBQ dinner at her home group for their cell group celebration. She included me into their group. I met many of our church members and also her parents. I had a very good time talking to them and eating very delicious food. I felt very comfortable and relaxed. Feroze, Anita's husband, barbequed so much meat and we ate it all. That was really fun.

The beginning of this year, 2012, I had to go to Credit Valley Hospital to check my stomach. I was told not to drive after the test and also told that I could not go by taxi, that somebody had to be with me. Unfortunately, my two trustees were busy that day and they could not take me to the hospital. I thought I would have to cancel the appointment. Then I remembered Anita, and called her and asked her. She said "yes" immediately and took me to the hospital and waited for me for a long time and drove me home safely. I was so thankful for her help and also thankful to God who sent me a beautiful sister in Him.

Anita and I met continually and thanked God and praised Him. Then one day God revealed to me the importance of thanksgiving and praise through Psalm 100. When I read:

Enter his gates with thanksgiving and his courts with praise; give thanks to him and praise his name. Psalm 100—4

He told me. "By what you are doing you are entering my gates and my courts with thanksgiving and praise." I was stunned because I did not know what I was doing. Then He showed me through my favourite Psalm 91. The Psalm 91 starts with 'He who dwells in the shelter of the Most High will rest in the shadow of the Almighty.' And there are so many wonderful promises of God to His children – His protection from plague, harm, disaster, and victory over enemies, and His promise of deliverance. He satisfies us with His salvation. I liked Psalm 91 so much that I memorized it years ago. But God showed me that all His promises are under one condition which is that we must dwell in the shelter of the Most High. I realized that we must get into His dwelling place by thanksgiving and praise.

I truly thanked God for His revelation about thanksgiving and praise. I was so thrilled about this experience, and determined to give thanks and praise to God in our meeting, knowing that one day we will say. "Better is one day in your courts than a thousand elsewhere."

On the 22nd of January, Pastor Faustin approached me and asked me.

"Akemi. Would you like to be a cell leader?"

"No, I don't."

"Pray about this please. Two more ladies want to join your group."

"New Season for My Art Work"

February 28, 2012

I started taking art courses at Visual Arts Mississauga a few years after I lost my husband. I took a water colour course for ten weeks in the spring, and ten weeks in the fall. I have been taking art courses for many years now. At first it was so difficult because I could not control the water, but I truly enjoy painting now.

When I paint I lose myself in painting. I enjoy colours, shapes, lights, and shades. I am in a totally different world recreating on the papers God's beautiful creations. I enjoyed painting and produced many water colour paintings. But I never sold one because they were like my own children, and I could not exchange my children for money. It's really silly, but I felt that way.

One Sunday last summer our church had a prophetic Sunday, and several artists brought their own art works and displayed them in the church. When I took some of my water colour paintings Margaret wanted to buy one of my paintings, but I could not sell it. I produced many paintings but I did not do anything about them.

On the 12th of February, when I went to the church Margaret approached me and asked me, "Akemi, I would really like to buy your painting. Could you sell it to me?"

"Margaret, I never sell my paintings because it's going to be very expensive when I frame it. Framing costs more than a 100 dollars," I said.

"You know I can't forget your paintings. They are so peaceful. I would really like to have one in my home."

When I heard that I changed my mind and said. "Margaret is it okay if I frame it by myself? I can buy a frame by myself and frame it. Is that okay?"

"Yes. It's okay."

"Which one do you like?"

"I would like to see them again."

"Okay. I will bring some of my paintings next Sunday. Do you like flowers or landscapes?"

"I like landscapes."

I decided to share my art works with Margaret. I painted all my paintings with God's help. If my paintings bring peace to someone I am very happy.

My neighbour Pat has two sons. The elder one moved out in January, and the younger one, Richard, moved back to his mom's house recently. One evening when I was cleaning the driveway Pat came out with a shovel and we talked for a while under snowflakes. I found out that Richard fell from the roof when he was working on the roof and broke his wrist and his ankle two years ago. He went through surgery, but his ankle did not heal perfectly. He decided to have another surgery. This time the doctor would break his ankle again and add a one-inch rod to his bone. Pat worried about Richard who would have to stay home for two months. I knew Richard likes art.

One day last summer I invited Pat and Richard to my house and showed my paintings hanging on the walls all over my house. Richard enjoyed and promised me to show me his art works, but it never happened. Pat said that when she told him to show his art works to me, he said, "No, its not good enough. I will show Akemi when I draw a good one."

I remembered all these things and said to Pat. "My husband left many textbooks from the Washington School of Art. They teach how to draw very neatly. Ken took a correspondence course before I met him. I will bring the books to Richard one day."

On the 15th of February, I went to De Serres, an art supply store, and bought a sketch book, pencils from B2 to B6, and a kneadable eraser, and visited Richard in the evening.

When I knocked on the door Pat came out and called Richard. I gave Richard my gifts and two art books, and told him. "There are 15 more text books, so when you finish one let me know."

Richard thanked me. Pat said. "When you finish one book, bring your works to Akemi. She will mark it for you."

"Oh no, I won't mark. Just enjoy, two months will go very quickly."

I gave a big hug to Richard and Pat and came home. I was so happy that I could help Richard in this way.

One day Flo Wingfelder, Janis Flower's mother, called me and asked me to fix two pairs of pants. Flo said to me. "Akemi, I want you to come and pick up the pants instead of giving them to my daughters. I want you to come around eleven and we will have lunch in the dining room."

I accepted her offer with thanks, and we set the date of the 20th of February, which was Family Day. A night before I called Flo and asked her if I could bring my art works from the last fall course, and she said that that would be nice. So I packed a few autumn leaves and portraits in my art case.

Flo is attending art classes at her condo, and every time I visit her she showed me her works at the classroom. She also showed me her friend's works too. It is so nice that old people enjoy art work regularly.

I drove to Joe and Filo's luxury condo. Flo was waiting for me at the entrance of the condo. We went to 1202 and enjoyed the beautiful view from the 12th floor. I showed my paintings to Joe and Flo, then Flo said, "Akemi can I call my friend Marcy to see your paintings?"

"That's fine with me."

Flo called Marcy, but she was tied up and could not come. Then Flo called another art friend, Doris, and she came. She enjoyed my paintings. It was so nice to meet another artist and I enjoyed it too.

Joe and Flo invited me to the dining room in the lobby and we had a good lunch. I drove home with two pairs of pants, and shortened them as soon as I came home.

I called Flo and thanked her for a wonderful Family Day that I spent with them. Then she said. "Akemi, please bring your art works again. I would like to show them to my friend Marcy."

"Yes I will. When you set the date let me know."

I was so glad that I could bring joy to the people with my art work, and at the same time thanked God that He can use anything I do for His glory.

Christmas gift from Linda

Jan 19, 2004

The Kindness of God on Good Friday

April 11, 2012

Good Friday's evening service was announced one week before the Easter Sunday in our church. I was excited about this plan, and thought that it would be so wonderful to spend a night with my brothers and sisters in the Lord, commemorating our Lord Jesus's death. Then I realized that I don't drive a car at night, but I would like so much to attend. It was quite disappointing, but I could attend the church on Easter morning, so it's okay to stay home on Friday night. That was my decision and I was satisfied with it.

On Wednesday morning Anita, a lady from our church, visited me. Anita and I had been meeting once every two weeks to spend time together in prayers, reading the Bible, and talking. When Anita came we talked about the Lord Jesus' death on the cross, and what He accomplished on the cross for us. We thanked Him and prayed that we would receive everything He prepared for us. We declared:

He was punished on the cross so that we might be forgiven.

He was wounded on the cross so that we might be healed.

He took all our sins on the cross so that we might share His righteousness.

He died our death on the cross so that we might live His life.

He took our rejection on the cross so that we might be called children of God.

He took our shame on the cross so that we might share His glory.

He took our poverty on the cross so that we might share His richness.

He took our curse on the cross so that we might share His blessings.

It was uplifting to know what is available for us through our Lord's death. We blessed each other and ended our meeting. Anita said. "Thank you, Akemi. I will see you on Friday evening at the church."

"I am not going there."

"Why not?"

"Anita. I really don't like to drive a car at night."

"I will take you there. I will call you before I leave my home."

"Really? Thank you so much."

We hugged each other and Anita drove home. That was a big surprise. "God thank you. I can attend the Good Friday service. You are so kind," I said.

On Friday morning, I woke up very early and finished the laundry and ate breakfast. Then suddenly the electricity went out. The last two years we had frequent blackouts on our street and sometimes it lasted more than ten hours. The last year from April to September Ontario Hydro undertook big construction on our street. It was a mess. I thought that we wouldn't have any more blackouts. I was so upset. I could not start sewing without power. I could not even open the garage door. I said to myself. "Now what? It's not a good way to start Good Friday." I decided to go out for a walk. I picked up two letters to mail and went out. The air was fresh and the grass was growing in the front yard of every house. Spring is here. I started feeling good. When I turned the corner, a car came from behind me and stopped beside me. The driver rolled down his window glass and said. "Hi Akemi, how are you?"

"I am fine Mark. How are you?"

"I am good, Akemi. Phyllis told me to tell you that the electricity will come back in an hour."

"Really? Thank you. That's good."

"Where are you going?"

"I would like to mail these letters. I can't even drive a car now."

"Why not?"

"I can't open the garage door."

"That's right. If you need my help let me know. Okay?"

"Thank you. Have a good day."

I was so relieved to know that the power would be back soon. I dropped the letters into the mailbox and walked in the park. I walked beside the community tennis court, and beside the public school, behind the school. I knew the trail so well. I had walked every day with tears after my husband Ken's death. But now I was walking with prayers and thanksgiving. I had good prayers.

When I came home the power was back on, and I found a message on my telephone. The message was from Justin Onzuka, a young man in our church. The message said, "Hi Akemi, this is Justin. I realized that you don't like to drive a car at night. If you want to go to the church tonight I will take you to the church, and bring you back. Call me." He left his phone number. I called him immediately and thanked him and told him that Anita would give me a ride. I was truly surprised. His kindness touched me deeply. I thanked God from the bottom of my heart. "Thank you, Father. You surround me with kind friends and I am so blessed."

In the afternoon, I received a call from our Pastor Faustin Fernando unexpectedly. He said, "Hi Akemi. How are you? This is Pastor Faustin.

"I am fine, thank you. How are you, Pastor Faustin?"

"I am good. Akemi, are you planning to come to the church this evening?"

"Yes I am. Anita will take me there."

"Oh good. It's good to know that. I will see you there."

"Thank you so much."

It was another surprise. I was so moved by Pastor Faustin's kindness. In his busy schedule he remembered me, and called me. I said. "Thank you, Father, you are so kind. You don't forget your widow and send me kind friends again and again. I feel so safe to live my life with your kindness and your protection." The tears started falling from my eyes.

Anita and her mother came to pick me up, and we attended the Good Friday service. I was so pleased that I was there because God wanted me to be there. The service was so good. I was overwhelmed by God's love for us. He gave us His only Son to die on the cross for us so that we can live full lives. Anita drove me home. That night I thanked God again and again for His kindness.

From the Older Adult Centre

April 14, 2012

One day in March I received a letter from my good friend, Dianne Schleifer. She wrote about the Older Adult Centre West which started in our neighbourhood. She recommended that I join it. It cost only ten dollars per year. She included a March schedule, and wrote on the schedule "You might be interested in a creative writing class."

I read the schedule. There were so many exercises, such as yoga, Tai Chi, chair exercise. When I read European Art History Impressionism, Monday 1:00-2:00, I just knew that I would enjoy one afternoon a week learning about art history. I drove to O.A.C. immediately and met Anne who is in charge of O.A.C. West and paid ten dollars and I joined the centre.

The following Monday I attended European Art History class. There were three other ladies and an instructor. Altogether five ladies watched a screen and learned about Impressionism. I really enjoyed one hour, but the screen was so bad. There were only two colours, black and ugly greenish yellow on the screen. We watched ugly colour for three weeks, and they changed to a bigger and beautiful screen.

In April, the creative writing class started. I hesitated to attend it, but it was only five weeks, and I wanted to learn about creative writing, so I decided to try it, even one class, and drove to the centre and registered for it. I found out that I was the first one to sign up. I really wondered if the class would start or not for just one person.

Water colour painting class was starting in April, and I would be so busy with homework. If I was the only student and had to write a story every week, I wondered if I could handle it or not. I almost regretted that I signed up for the creative writing class.

The night before the creative writing class started I really prayed to God about the class. I said. "Father, I am going to attend the creative writing class tomorrow. If it's for me bless it abundantly, and if it's not for me let me know clearly. Thank you."

The class was from 11:45 am to 12:45 pm. On the first of April, I drove to the O.A.C. around 11:30 am and waited in the small church library, but nobody came. Anne came to the library and was with me for a short time, but I was all alone and just waited and waited. I waited until 12:30 pm and said to Anne, "I am hungry. I will go home," and drove home. I thought that God showed me clearly it wasn't for me.

But for some reason the next Monday, April the 8th, I wanted to try one more time. This time I packed a simple lunch and drove to the O.A.C. again. When I arrived, Anne was there and greeted me. "Good to see you. Teacher is here today, and two more ladies signed for the class."

"That's really nice," I said.

I went to the small church library again but nobody was there, but a jacket and a bag were on the sofa. Meanwhile a lady came into the room and asked me. "Are you the one who is taking creative writing class?"

"Yes I am. Are you my teacher?"

"Yes I am. I am Anthazia."

"Glad to meet you. I am Akemi."

We waited for other ladies to come, but nobody showed up.

Anthazia told me that she has published two books, and has a passion for writing. I told her that I don't write fiction but I have been writing essays about the goodness of God in my life for about twelve years, and took out a couple of "Akemi's Journals" from my bag and showed them to her.

We waited but nobody joined us so Anthazia started teaching about creative writing, and gave me a paper to write a story. I wrote a plan but could not write a story, so I promised her to write one story by next class. When I was planning my next story Anthazia read my journal, and said suddenly, "Let's publish your journal. I have a friend who publishes books. I will contact her. Let's do it."

I could not believe what I heard.

"Really? I met a lady who is going to publish her books. She said to me that she paid 7,000 dollars," I said.

"No, it's not that expensive. I will talk to my friend and let you know. Do you have more journals?"

"Yes I do."

"Bring them over next Monday."

I truly thanked her, and she left.

I had a quick lunch and attended European Art History class in the afternoon. I could not believe what just happened. I said to myself. "Is it really true that I am going to publish my book?"

I never told anybody, but writing a book was my only dream since I was a young girl. I never wanted to be a teacher or a nurse, or a secretary. I just wanted to write beautiful stories. I was totally shocked.

The following day, April the 2nd, the water colour class started at Visual Arts Mississauga. I had homework from the creative writing class and also the art class. I had such a busy week, but I wrote one essay and prepared for the next class.

On the next Monday, I packed all my journals, my homework and lunch in a bag, and was very excited to attend the second class. While I was in the backyard, Anne from O.A.C. left a message and informed me that the creative writing class was cancelled. I was shocked and bitterly disappointed. So, my book is not going to be published after all. It was a very short sweet dream.

I attended the European Art History class and had a relaxed time with the ladies. When I met Anne I asked. "Anne, about the creative writing class, is it cancelled totally or just today?"

"Only this week. You will have a class next Monday."

I was relieved, but realized that I should not expect too much any more.

However, at the following class when I arrived at the library, Anthazia was already there and told me to write the foreword, the acknowledgement, and my own history for my book. She taught about creative writing more and our class ended.

During the week I wrote the foreword, acknowledgement, and my short history. I prepared my photo too.

The last week, Anthazia asked me to write the conclusion of my book. She extended one more week just for me. I realized that my book "Akemi's Journal" will be published someday.

I attended the creative writing class at the O.A.C. and this unexpected thing had happened. I was the only student in the class all the time as if God arranged the class for me. I remembered my prayer to God. "Father, I am going to attend the creative writing class tomorrow. If it's for me bless it abundantly, and if it's not for me let me know clearly." He blessed me abundantly more than I expected. Thank you, Father.

We Had a Guest Speaker

June 7, 2012

I have been attending Catch the Fire Mississauga for about two and a half years since the opening day. When I started going there, Pastor Faustin Fernando and his wife, Marina, invited me to join the intercession group, people who pray for our church one hour before the service starts. The church service starts at 10:30 am so I go to the church at 9:30 am.

Since I joined the group many things have changed; some people left, and new people joined. I continually went to the church at 9:30 am and prayed. First, I really worried about what to pray, but soon found out that there was always something God gave to me to pray for, and I thanked God for that. Now we have a very small group of five, Pastor Faustin, Marina, Rodorigo, his wife Liliana, and myself. The last two and a half years lots of thanksgiving, praises, and also lots of petitions went up to Heaven. I am so blessed to be a part of this group. We are using the drama room of the West Credit Secondary School for our prayer room.

On the 20th of May, I went to the church a little before 9:30 am, and went to the room where we pray. I arranged the chairs and thanked God. Then Marina came and said "Good morning Akemi. Rodorigo is not coming today. We are the only ones this morning."

That Sunday Pastor Faustin was in India on a mission trip. Marina and I prayed for God's blessing over our church. When we finished our prayers, Marina said "Let's go to the worship room. Mark is already there, let's pray over him."

Since Pastor Faustin was away we had a guest speaker on that Sunday, Mark. He is a son of our friend Ellie Murack, and he is a pastor of a church in Peterborough. Ellie and Mark and his wife came to the church very early and went to the room where we worship.

"Marina why don't you invite him here. This room is quieter

than there," I said. The worship team were practicing there.

"Okay, I will do that." Marina went out from the room and soon came back with Ellie and Mark. The four of us stood up and held hands together and prayed.

While each one of us was offering his or her prayers to God, suddenly Mark knelt on his knees. When our prayers came to a stop, Mark looked at me straight in my eyes and said. "This lady is full of grace. Would you put your hand over me and pray for me?"

I could not believe what I heard. I had to digest what he said. Mark was still looking at me on his knees. "Me? Do you want me to pray over you?"

"Yes. Please."

"What do I do?" I asked because nobody had asked me this kind of request before.

"Lay your hand over me and bless me."

I did as Mark requested. I did not know how to pray, but as soon as I put my hand over his head words came to me. I asked God to increase His grace over him, and simply bless his life with God and his wonderful future. Mark thanked me. I still could not believe what just happened. I was so shocked and at the same time filled with awe. "God is this real? What is happening here?" I said in my heart. So many things have happened in the intercession room, but I never experienced this kind of surprise.

The service started, the worship was beautiful and Mark's teaching was great. He emphasized the importance of being God's friend instead of doing something for God, and I totally agreed with him.

After the service, many people went to Mark and he prayed over them. When the last person was prayed for by Mark, I went to him and thanked him. "Thank you for coming to our church. I am so glad I met you."

"I am glad I met you! I wanted to tell you that your word has power and authority. This morning while we were praying I sensed that your name is well known in Heaven more than on earth."

I was shocked again by his comment. I did not have any words and just said, "Thank you."

Mark took my hands with his both hands and blessed me. It was truly an awesome experience. I came home with an astonishing feeling as if I experienced Jesus' transfiguration on the mount or I saw a glimpse of Heaven. I just thanked God. I did not know what else to do.

The following Sunday Ellie came to me and gave me a big hug.

"Ellie, you have a wonderful son. I am so grateful that I met him," I said.

"Oh Akemi, Mark was so thrilled to receive a prayer from you. He was so excited about meeting you. He said that was the reason he visited our church, and also said that your name is well known in Heaven more than on earth."

I was shocked again by her comment.

I came home from the church and fixed a simple lunch, and took it into my backyard. I ate my lunch in the garden surrounded by the perennials which were growing healthily. It was so peaceful. I thanked God from the bottom of my heart for creating me, taking me into His family, and promising me a wonderful life in Heaven. "Your Will be done, Lord. All Your plans and dreams for my life will be fulfilled."

I will certainly cherish this beautiful experience as long as I live, and it will encourage me tremendously on my life's journey.

My Cataract Surgery

July 6, 2012

Last summer I started sensing difficulty in my right eye. Everything looked too bright and I felt very uncomfortable. When I visited my eye doctor, Dr. Ahmed, I mentioned to her about my right eye. Then she checked it carefully and said, "You have a cataract in your right eye, and you need surgery immediately. We will contact you soon."

A few days later a lady from the office called me and asked me if I would like to have my eye surgery in Toronto or Mississauga. She also told me if I had surgery in Toronto I had to wait for three months, but if in Mississauga I had to wait for a year. After I talked to Janis Flowers, one of my trustees, I decided to have surgery in Toronto. I called the office, and the lady made an appointment for me.

On the 24th of August, 2011, Janis drove me to Toronto, and I met the doctor in the gorgeous office. He explained to me about the surgery. After I talked to the doctor I was sent to another office on the third floor to book my surgery date.

A young lady talked to me and said, "It will cost 1,250 dollars."

I said, "I asked the doctor about the cost, and he said it's free. It's covered by OHIP."

"Oh, if you do your surgery in a hospital it's free, but if you do it in this building it costs $1,250. It has to be an authorized cheque or a credit card." I did not mind spending money for my eye, but I did not feel comfortable at all. I needed time to think about it. Janis and I went out for lunch, but I realized that I needed surgery anyway. We came back to the office and booked the surgery date on the 6th of October.

Janis drove me home. The traffic was heavy and it was a long drive. I started regretting my decision to do the surgery in Toronto.

That night I prayed about my eye surgery in Toronto but I did not have any peace. I just knew that I made a mistake. But what could I do? I asked God to bless my eye surgery and send me good helpers to go through it.

Two weeks later my good friend, Anita, invited me unexpectedly to her and her husband Feroze's cell group barbeque dinner. I wasn't a member of their group, but she included me into their group. Anita picked me up and drove me to their home in Streetsville. Feroze and Anita have a big and beautiful home, and their backyard is so huge, also there is a park next to their backyard.

There were already about a dozen people from our church, and I felt very comfortable. We had plenty of barbeque dinner and we enjoyed each other. I was introduced to Anita's parents for the first time. They are very nice people from Guyana, and I truly enjoyed talking to them. I found out that Anita's father is a retired school principal. I told him that my father was a principal of an elementary school in Japan many years ago.

I was so comfortable to be with them that I told them that I was going to have a cataract surgery in Toronto in a month. Then both of them said that they had cataract surgeries from Dr. Vettese at the Credit Valley Hospital. They recommended me to have my surgery by Dr. Vettese. Anita's father gave me a doctor's card and said to me, "Bring this card to your eye doctor and ask them to switch your surgery to Mississauga. Dr. Vettese is a very good doctor." I truly thanked them and decided to do my surgery in Mississauga with Dr. Vettese. Then immediately peace came back to my heart, and made me so happy. I thanked Anita for inviting me to her barbeque dinner party, and also thanked God for His guidance in my eye surgery. He gave me a new doctor.

A few days later I visited Dr. Ahmed's office with Dr. Vettese's card and asked the lady to change my surgery from Toronto to Mississauga. The lady said that she would take care of this matter. I came home with such peace and great relief. I did not have to ask anybody to visit the doctor's office since I can drive myself, and if I can't I can call a taxi. It's much easier than Toronto. I thanked God from the bottom of my heart.

On the 14th of March, I visited Dr. Vettese's office for the first time and met him. He is a very gentle and kind doctor, and I felt so comfortable talking to him. I told him my situation. "I lost my husband twelve years ago, and I don't have any children, so I have to ask my trustee to help me. It's not convenient for me to have someone to stay overnight on my surgery day. Also my trustee is away for six weeks from April to May. My surgery has to be at the end of May or June."

"Tell the same thing to my secretary and set the date."

"Thank you so much. I feel much better now. It's not easy to live in a foreign land without a husband and children, and with poor English."

"I don't know about poor English. Your English is good." He smiled at me. I was so glad I changed the doctor, and thanked God for His help.

I had to visit Dr. Vettese's office twice and twice at the hospital for the test, but I was able to go by myself, and I was so happy about it.

The surgery date was set for the 14th of June. Many of my friends who had cataract surgery previously kindly told me things I should not do after surgery like … do not bend, do not carry heavy things, do not wash hair, do not cook … I thought that I can't live like that. But I prepared everything I could. I cooked many dishes and froze them. I cleaned the garden and house and did laundry. When the date was set Anita offered to take me to the hospital, and Janis offered to stay overnight.

On the 14th of June, Anita came at 6:30 am and drove me to the hospital. We waited for a long time and I talked to two ladies to prepare my document, but the actual surgery took only 10 to 15 minutes. After the surgery Anita drove me to her home and picked up chicken soup which her mother cooked for me, and drove me home. I ate delicious chicken soup for lunch. That night Janis stayed with me. I felt so secure. The next day my neighbour Darline drove me to Dr. Vettese's office.

We had to wait about an hour, so we talked a lot, and I came to know her closely. I was blessed to have such a kind neighbour.

Anita delivered meals to me for about 10 days. I was so spoiled.

Four days after the surgery I started feeling pressure on my right eye and severe pain on my right neck and shoulder. I made an appointment with Dr. Vettese and went to see him on the 27th of June. He kindly took me in and checked my eye. He said, "Your eye is perfect. Do not worry about pain. Come and see me next week too." I was so relieved.

The following week I visited Dr. Vettese again. He was very pleased with the result of my surgery. "Your eye is perfect. Continue to use eye drops for the next two weeks and at the end of this month visit your eye doctor to change your glasses."

I thanked him and drove home happily.

When I arrived home, I called Anita to thank her, but she wasn't there. Instead I talked to her mother. She was so pleased with my good report and said, "Dr. Vettese is a good doctor, right?"

"Yes he is. I am very thankful that you recommended him to do my surgery. Thank you for your help. Thank you for cooking delicious food for me."

I really thanked God for helping me in wonderful ways; giving me a good doctor, surrounded me with good helpers. He truly meets all my needs more than I can think. My pain is getting better each day, and I am thankful for that too.

Precious Day in the Summer of 2012

July 22, 2012

On the 11th of July, my good friend Rita called me and told me that she was free from her work the following week, and asked me if I wanted to do something with her. I said, "That would be very nice. I would like to invite Marlene for lunch one day."

"That's a good idea. Let's do it," replied Rita.

"When is a good time for you?" I asked.

"Call Marlene and ask her and let me know," suggested Rita.

I called Marlene Traas and found out she was free any day of the coming week. I contacted Rita again and decided to have lunch on the 16th of July. I called Marlene and told her that Rita and I would pick her up at 11 am on the next Monday.

Marlene just moved to a senior home in Oakville from Waterdown. She used to live in a huge luxury condo with her husband, Mac, but he developed dementia and moved to a nursing home many years ago, and passed away last May. Marlene faced so many difficulties in her life. I wanted to be with her badly, and Rita would help me. It was such a blessing for me.

On the 16th of July, I woke up at 5:30 am. I was so excited about having lunch with Marlene and Rita that I could not go back to sleep! I got up and changed my clothes, made the bed, went outside and watered the garden. Then I started cutting the vegetables, and set the table for our lunch. I finished most of the preparation by 7:30 am, and I was very pleased. I prayed to God to bless our gathering and invited Him to be with us. I was so excited to have Marlene and Rita in my house.

Rita came to my home at 10:30 am, and we went to Oakville to pick up Marlene. When we arrived, Marlene was ready to go out. Rita drove us back to my home. I prepared lunch and soon we ate lunch in my living room, because it was a hot and humid day. We really enjoyed eating lunch together.

After lunch Marlene wanted to go out to the garden. It was quite a hot day, but we were able to sit on the garden chairs under the wisteria tree, and spent time together surrounded by the beautiful blooming summer flowers.

It was 23 years ago Marlene, Rita and I met at the ladies Bible study, Coffee Break at the Community Church in Meadowvale. Marlene was one of the leaders, and I was looking after coffee and tea for the ladies. Rita started coming to the Coffee Break with her daughter Julia. She was only 3 years old then.

I went to the church about 30 minutes earlier and prepared coffee and tea, and put the mugs on the tray for about 30 ladies. After the Bible study, I cleaned all the mugs and coffee and tea pots by myself. Every time I was cleaning the mugs and pots Rita came with Julia and helped me. Nobody came, but she came and helped me so faithfully. I remembered so many things like it was yesterday.

We talked about the old days. Then Marlene said, "When I was watching Akemi washing mugs the Lord spoke to me 'That is my precious daughter' so I went to you and introduced myself."

We all were so amazed that our friendship was planned by God 23 years ago. God sent these precious sisters into my life 23 years ago. Since then they have been such wonderful sisters in the Lord and showed me His love again and again.

On the day I lost my husband, Ken, Marlene visited me and stayed overnight with me, and the next day she drove me to the funeral home to plan Ken's funeral. She also printed my journal many times. Those were awesome gifts for me and made me so happy.

Rita also visited me faithfully once a week after Ken's death and prayed over me with powerful prayers. God arranged our friendship 23 years ago, and we are still good friends. I thought that our friendship will continue to eternity. We will be enjoying each other in Heaven too. We really have blessed lives.

We talked about the past, present and future in the peaceful garden. Marlene shared with us what she was experiencing in her life now, many difficulties and sorrows. Rita and I prayed over her and declared for her a bright future with the Lord.

Rita drove us again to the senior's home in Oakville, and we said goodbye to Marlene. While we were coming home I was so pleased with what we did that day. Joy bubbled up in my heart and stayed there for a long time. I sensed that God was pleased with what we did for His precious daughter Marlene, and said to me, "Thank you. You did a good job. I am very pleased!" I thanked God again and again in my heart. It made me so happy. We will do it again, I said in my heart. I also thanked Rita for driving us and her kind heart.

Crocus from Janis

Jan 18, 2004

My 75th Birthday
October 2, 2012

One night in early October while I was lying on my bed I was filled with thanksgiving towards God who rescued me and helped me my whole life. I just thanked God in my heart again and again, and said, "Lord, thank you for being with me. I am so blessed," and I added "by the way my 75th birthday is coming soon. Would you give me a wonderful birthday?" then I fell asleep.

One day my good friend, Rita, said to me, "Akemi, we are planning your birthday, but we don't want to go to a restaurant, because we really want to bless you. Can we come to your home?"

"Of course you can," I said, "Thank you so much. You can use my home and my china. It's really nice. I don't have to go out."

Rita told me that some ladies were coming to my house with food. That was very thoughtful. I thanked her for their kindness.

On the 7th of October at our church, when the Sunday service ended, somebody tapped on my shoulder. When I looked back Christine and her mother, Valentine, were standing there, and they said.

"Akemi. We would like to take you out for dinner this coming Saturday evening."

"What?" I was truly shocked. One week before Christine said to me. "Your birthday is coming soon Akemi."

"How do you know it?"

"I read your journal. That's why I remember your birthday."

One evening last summer Christine visited me, and I taught her how to paint in water colour for about an hour, and we had a good time together. When she left she took one of my journals.

Now Christine and her mother were inviting me for dinner.

"Thank you so much. This is really a big surprise."

By then Christine's father Joe joined us. I said to him. "Joe thank you so much. This is wonderful. I am not going to ask you why?" Everybody laughed. They said that they will call me before they leave their house. It was truly a big surprise. I could not believe what just happened.

On the 12th of October, two days before my birthday, five ladies, Rita, Heather, Diane, Anita and Norma came with food and drinks, and celebrated my birthday at my home. They did everything in the kitchen. I enjoyed good company and good food. I was served a beautifully decorated cake with "Happy 75th Birthday Akemi" on it. They did everything by themselves and even cleaned the kitchen very neatly. Then they said, "Akemi, we would like to bless you. You sit on that chair and we will pray over you."

I sat on the chair and the ladies stood around me and prayed and prophesied over me. They really blessed me. I felt God was touching me through these faithful ladies. When they finished their prayers, God touched everyone and blessed everyone. God joined my birthday party. I thanked the ladies for a wonderful birthday party and thanked God for what He gave to me.

On the 13th of October, Christine and her parents picked me up and we drove to a restaurant called Twin Fish at the corner of Hurontario and Courtneypark Drive. The restaurant was owned by two Christians. It was a very small restaurant, but very clean and it was packed with customers. It was the first time I was to dine there. I enjoyed the cleanliness of the restaurant and soft Christian music in the air. I ordered red snapper fillet with rice. I enjoyed dining with Joe's family. They took me into their family. That was so special for me, and also the red snapper was very tasty.

When they drove me home I invited them into my house and offered them a cup of tea, and showed them my paintings. It was a wonderful birthday dinner. I truly thanked Joe's family and God from the bottom of my heart.

On the 14th of October, on my birthday, I went to our church, Catch the Fire Mississauga, very early in the morning to pray. Then Liliana came and asked me, "Good morning Akemi. Did you have a good week?"

"Yes I did," I said. "My friends celebrated my birthday."

"When was your birthday?"

"Today."

"Congratulations."

"Thank you."

Liliana told her husband about my birthday, and he told Pastor Marina about it.

During the service Marina invited me to the front and blessed me. She also asked people "If anyone has a prophecy for Akemi please speak out." Several people gave me a prophetic word, and everybody sang "Happy Birthday to you." That was a big surprise. I was blessed by the whole church.

When I came home Janis Flowers had left a message. "Happy Birthday Akemi. Selam and I would like to take you to Swiss Chalet for dinner this evening. Please call me." I called her and accepted her invitation.

Janis and Selam took me out for dinner and we enjoyed the meal and our time together. We came back to my home and Janis made tea for us while I was shortening Selam's two pairs of pants.

That night I really thanked God for the wonderful birthday He gave to me. He gave me a birthday party and two dinners. He sent me beautiful people and celebrated my birthday more than I ever expected. He showed His love and kindness through my good friends. "Lord, I asked you to give me a wonderful birthday, and you truly blessed me. Thank you so much. You are so good."

On the 16th of October, Pastor Faustin called me unexpectedly. He said, "Happy Birthday Akemi."

"Thank you."

"I missed your birthday on Sunday. I would like to take you out for lunch tomorrow. I would like to go to the Sushi restaurant you mentioned before."

"Thank you so much, but I don't like to go out tomorrow." I declined his offer because he is a very busy person and I did not want him to do anything for me.

"Then I will come to your place with sushi tomorrow. What time do you eat lunch?"

"Well, thank you. I eat lunch around one o'clock."

"Then I will be at your place a quarter to one. See you tomorrow."

"Thank you." I said. I could not believe what just happened.

The following day at 12:45 pm Pastor Faustin came with sushi take out and spent about one hour eating sushi lunch. We had good fellowship and talked about nothing but the goodness of God in our lives. It was truly uplifting and also the most unexpected birthday lunch God gave me. I thanked Pastor Faustin and also God deeply.

"Thank you Lord, You are truly amazing."

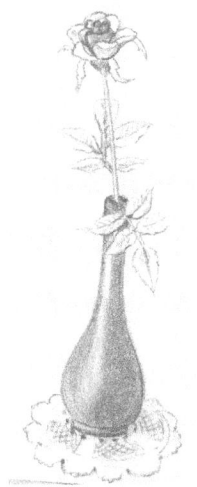

The New Fence

November 17, 2012

About two years ago my neighbour Stephanie said to me, "I would like to have a new fence. This fence is really old. Could you pay half of it?"

"Of course I will. I would like to have a new fence too," I replied.

The fence was already 33 years old. Once it fell down, and my husband fixed it, but he used the same material. I was excited about having a new fence and waited for the day to come, but she never said anything about the fence again.

Last summer I saw Stephanie painting the fence with black paint. She has a black deck and even the soil in her front yard is black. I visited her and said. "Hi Stephanie, you are working hard. Aren't you going to build a new fence?"

"Oh well, you know we had to fix lots of things in our house and did not have enough money for the fence."

So I continued to have a wobbling old fence. Every time a strong wind blew Gary called me and asked me, "Akemi is your fence alright? Did it not fall down?"

"It's still there. Thank you." I answered.

But this summer we had a very strong wind one night, and the next morning the fence was damaged badly. Two panels were missing and the bottom part of the wood had fallen down. I tried to push back the bottom wood, but it was too heavy for me. It was on a Saturday so I called Gary and mentioned about the fence. He came to see the fence in the late morning and said, "Akemi, you need a new fence."

"That's good. Could you find someone?"

"Sure, I will ask my aunt. She knows someone."

"Gary, I need a new deck too."

"Oh yeah, this is not safe any more."

The deck was slanted badly. Gary jumped up and down on the deck, and the deck moved quite a bit.

"Don't do that Gary. I still need this deck."

One Saturday morning in August Gary invited a carpenter, Jerry, and introduced me. Jerry looked at my deck and fence carefully. I told him that I did not need the front side of the fence, just wanted to have the side, and also talked about the style of the deck. Jerry listened to me and understood my desires. A few days later Jerry called Gary and told him the price.

A couple of days later Gary and I visited my neighbour, and Jeffrey, Stephanie's husband was there. Gary mentioned about putting up a new fence. Then he said to us. "I don't get a pay check every other week or every month. When I get it it's a lot. I have to tell Stephanie about it."

A few days later while I was in the backyard Stephanie said to me that she wanted to fix her backyard fence too.

Since then nothing happened. The fence looked awful, more panels came down. There was a big hole, and it looked like a slum. I did not like it at all. The summer went by, and I did not hear anything from Jerry either. But one day Gary told me that Jerry would come in October and let us know the date of the work one week before. I was so glad to know that!

Then one day Stephanie came to me while I was in the front yard, and said to me. "Could you wait building the fence for two more months? I can't afford it right now. We had to fix a water leak upstairs and I need a new dryer."

"Stephanie, I would like to build the fence as soon as possible," I replied. "I will pay the full price and you can pay me back whenever you are able to. That's good for me."

On the 17th of October, Gary called me from the office and told me that Jerry would come next Monday. I told my neighbour about it, and Gary came on the 20th to cut my yew tree and bridal wreath to make room for the workers.

On the 22nd of October when I came home from art class a big truck was on my driveway, and two men were working. The old deck and fence were already removed completely. I said hello to Jerry and his helper and went into the house. They worked very hard and put new poles in the ground by the evening. I paid half the amount of money to Jerry, and they left. The following day it rained all day, but Wednesday was a fine day. I took my car out and opened the garage door very early in the morning. Jerry and his helper worked so hard for the next two days. Everything was perfect. I enjoyed watching my new deck and fence being built skillfully, except a fuse went out twice. Fortunately, I was at home so that I could fix it. I also went to TD Bank for two days to withdraw money because Jerry preferred cash.

By Thursday evening almost all the work was done. Jerry said that he would finish it on Friday. I truly thanked them for the good work.

That night while I was lying on my bed, suddenly a thought came to my mind to ask Jerry to cut down my old apple tree. The tree was growing so big and making too much shade on the flower garden, and also I could not eat any apples any more because I don't spray it.

The next morning when Jerry came I said, "Good morning Jerry. Can you cut down my old apple tree?"

"Where is it?"

"In my backyard."

We went to the backyard.

"Do you want me to clean up the branches?"

"Yes I do."

"Okay."

"How much?"

"Well how about 250 dollars."

"That's good. Please cut it down."

After I paid for the deck and the fence I had exactly 250 dollars cash. I was so glad.

They cut the apple tree and fixed my neighbour's fence and finished all their work by three o'clock in the afternoon. They washed the new deck and the driveway with water. I was so happy to see my front yard.

"Thank you so much. You did a good job." I said.

"You know you saved lots of money. I never thought it would take that long." Jerry said.

"I am very thankful."

"I lost lots of money."

"Well, you are okay because you are a rich man."

"I am not a rich man."

"Yes you are. Thank you so much."

We both laughed and said good-bye. When they drove the big truck away, I drove my car into the garage. Then it started raining immediately. It rained for the whole week. I was so pleased that they had finished their work before the rain.

I have a brand new deck and a brand new fence, also my back yard has more sunshine for the flowers. I already look forward to next spring. I really thanked God for everything.

Christmas Gift from Our Heavenly Father

January 5, 2013

Our church had many equipping nights this fall with guest speakers who taught us. On the 27th of November, we had Isabel Allum, a prophetess, as a guest speaker. Fortunately, Joe Lobo, a gentleman in our church offered me a ride so that I was able to attend that evening.

After a short worship, Isabel taught us the difference between the gift of prophecy and the spirit of prophecy. It was really interesting teaching. After her teaching, she and two more people who came with her started to prophesy over each one of us.

I waited for a long time but my time came. Joe allowed me to use his cell phone to record her prophecy. Isabel asked me my name and said, "You have wonderful faith and a pure heart. You learn, learn and learn from everything. You have lots of testimonies of what God does in your life. You lifted burdens from many people, and God will reward you in public. God has a wonderful Christmas gift for you. He will dump it on your lap. It is coming like heavy rain. You went through many fires and never complained. He will reward you in public."

The prophecy was so excellent that I could not believe she was talking to me! I was astonished! I asked God in my heart, "God, do you really see me like that? It is an honour. Thank you."

I became so curious about the Christmas gift from the Lord, and was so excited about the gift as if I was a little girl waiting for a Christmas gift. Isabel said that 'God will drop it on your lap,' and it is 'like a heavy rain.' I could hardly wait for His Christmas gift.

On the 23rd of December, right after I came back from the

church, Nan visited me with her son Daniel. Years ago, I met Daniel at the Community Church. As a little boy Daniel always sat beside me every Sunday, and we did origami together. I truly enjoyed him. After I left the church I kept on sending a birthday card on his birthday and prayed every morning for his bright future with God's blessing and His favour. Since I don't have my own children I don't have grandchildren, but Daniel became like my own grandson, and I was so excited about praying for him every morning.

Daniel brought his sketch book and his cell phone which registered many photos he had taken. He showed me his sketches and pictures in his cell phone with his explanation. I truly enjoyed spending time with him. He also brought me a beautiful Christmas card. In it was written,

"Best wishes.

Thank you for all you have done over the years."

I was so happy to receive the neatly written card from Daniel. I thought that was a wonderful Christmas gift from the Lord.

On the 24th of December, only one day before Christmas, my publisher Cheryl Xavier's husband called me and said, "I am supposed to deliver your books today, but my car does not start. Could you come and pick them up?"

"What is your address?" I asked. He started telling me his address and how to get there, but I was so confused. I said, "You know, I am already lost. I will check a map and find out. I will call you before I leave."

It was easy to find out and soon I drove there. Mr. Xavier loaded my books into my car. I drove home safely. I was so happy, and also excited. I wanted to write a book so badly when I was 20 years old, but I did not tell anybody about my secret desire. I did not tell God about it. After 55 years, God fulfilled my dream. It was so special. When I moved all my books to the kitchen table, little by little, I almost cried. "Lord you finally published books for me. You are so wonderful. I can't still believe it's really happened." I carried all my books to the sunroom upstairs, and put them into two boxes.

I thought these books were truly a wonderful Christmas gift from God.

In the evening Gary visited me with a Christmas gift. I added my brand-new book into his gift bag. My first book was given to Gary, and I was so pleased. Gary was happy to see my book and said, "Thank you. You must feel good about it. You've accomplished something."

"Yes, it was my old dream, so I am very thankful."

I showed him my own sketches in the book. We talked for a while, and when he was about to go from my house he said to me, "Don't you ever think about moving to an old age home. Akemi, I want you to die in this house." After he left I started crying softly. I said to God, "Thank you Father. I am surrounded by kind people. I don't have to worry about getting older. This is the best Christmas gift from you."

I made two parcels, one for my sister in Japan and one for my friend Ingrid in Germany, and sent two books to them.

On Christmas day, I was invited for a dinner with Carol Hay, but she was recovering from being sick and her husband and her daughter were sick, so I decided to stay home. I had a very quiet Christmas by myself, but my heart was full of thanksgiving towards our wonderful Heavenly Father.

Christmas was over, but I was still expecting another wonderful gift from God. "Father if you still have a wonderful gift for me, I am happy to receive it."

The night of the 26th of December it started snowing. On the 27th morning I woke up around 6:30 and heard a faint sound of shovelling on my driveway. Wondering what was going on on my driveway, I put on a gown, walked to the sunroom next to my bedroom, and looked down at the driveway. I saw my neighbour's young man, Richard, cleaning my driveway. The snow was so thick and Richard was shovelling vigorously. I decided to thank him later and went back to bed. I slept again and woke up an hour later. I wanted to see the beautiful white world, so I put on the gown again and went to the sunroom. I looked down at the snow covered white street. Many people were shovelling their driveways, and Erwin was shovelling his driveway. While I was enjoying watching the pure white world a red car came and slowed down in front of my home. It stopped in front of Erwin's driveway. A man in the car talked with Erwin for awhile and drove to the end of the street and came back again. While I was watching the car the man waved at me. I waved back without knowing who he was. Then soon my phone rang.

"Hello," I said.

"Akemi, how are you?" Gary said.

"I am fine. Thank you."

"You did not clean your driveway, did you?"

"No, I didn't. Richard did it for me."

"I came here to clean your driveway, but it's already done. You have a good day Akemi."

"Thank you, Gary. You have a good day too."

My friends were so kind to me. My heart was filled with thanksgiving.

"Father thank you so much. You look after me so well. This is another wonderful gift from You. The gifts are truly like heavy rain, and my lap is full of Your gifts. Thank you so much. I am so blessed."

It is so good to be a child of God and receive wonderful gifts from our Heavenly Father.

"Goodbye Eleanore"

February 12, 2013

I attended Eleanore Sproule, my English teacher's, funeral on the 22nd of January. My good friend Janette and her husband drove to the Meadowvale Cemetery. Many of her friends and family got together and celebrated her life with beautiful music and heartfelt farewell speeches. I felt so cold that I put on my winter coat in the room. I had known Eleanore more than 14 years, and received so many blessings from her. Sitting on the cold chair I did not know how to think or feel. My mind was totally numb.

Soon my mind drifted back to the day I first met Eleanore. It was at Wake Up Call, ladies Bible study, at Toronto Airport Christian Fellowship. A neatly dressed lady sat beside me. I had never seen her at the Wake Up Call before. I turned to her and said, "Hello, I am Akemi."

"Hello, I am Eleanore," she said with a beautiful smile, and she added, "I am a teacher." That made my curiosity rise high. We don't usually tell our occupation on the first time we meet. I asked her, "What kind of teacher are you?"

"I teach English as a second language," she replied. Eleanore told me that she was teaching many young people from non-English speaking countries. I also learned that she visited students' homes to teach them. I was so curious that I asked her again, "Do you teach adults too?"

"Yes, I do," she answered.

That day as soon as I arrived home I told my husband. "I met a wonderful lady at Wake Up Call today. She teaches English as a second language. Can I take English lessons from her?" I asked, and added, "I am not asking you for a fur coat or diamond ring. Is that okay?"

"Of course it's okay, but how can you visit her?" he enquired.

"I don't have to go anywhere. She will visit me," I told him.

The next time I met Eleanore I officially asked her to teach me English and gave her my address.

Eleanore started visiting me and teaching English from the basics. She gave me lots of homework. Every time she visited me she brought one book to read and asked me to write a book report on it. She also gave me ten new words and I wrote ten sentences using the new words. Soon I realized that taking English lessons wasn't just one day a week work but six days work. Soon Eleanore brought a notebook and asked me to write an essay and present it every time she visited. I asked her to visit me once every two weeks because I could not handle it well. She visited me once every two weeks. Soon I started writing about the goodness of God in my life, and truly enjoyed it.

When I started English lessons, my husband, Ken, was still alive and he met Eleanore, but soon I lost him. After Ken's death Eleanore looked after me so well. She and her husband, Keith, attended Ken's memorial service and comforted me.

After Ken's death, I could not do anything so I did not take English lessons for a long time. Later I started again and wrote about my husband's death and my grief. That helped me so much! I received tremendous healing from writing essays.

One day Eleanore invited me and my friend Molly for lunch at her home. Molly drove me there. We ate delicious food which Keith cooked for us. I had a wonderful time with them. Their kindness touched my heart deeply.

Soon I started taking water colour classes at Visual Arts Mississauga, and asked Eleanore to visit me once every three weeks. Since I enjoyed having Eleanore at my home so much, and also I received so much joy by writing essays, I could not stop it. Years went by, and I wrote so many essays and Eleanore checked them thoroughly.

One day in January 2011, Eleanore called me and informed me

that she could not drive the car anymore. She had developed Lou Gehrig's disease, and she asked me to visit her home for my English lessons, but I could not do that. I did not want to drive that far. It was really sad, because I wanted to write about the goodness of God continually. I asked her if I could send my essays to her, and she said it was okay, she would mark them for me. I was so relieved and kept on writing and sending my essays to her. It lasted about two years until her death.

I learned so much from Eleanore, not only English but also how to live my life. She was truly an amazing person who always talked about the positive side of everything. She never looked at the negative side, never looked at a half empty glass, but a half full glass. She often said, "God is good." She lived her life with God's blessing.

Unexpectedly I published my book, *Akemi's Journals*, and one day before Christmas I received them. I was so pleased and wanted to bring one to Eleanore. My friend, Rita, drove me to Eleanore's home on the 10th of January, and I presented my book to her. She was very pleased.

Only eight days later Eleanore passed away. She went to Heaven. I was so pleased that she was totally free, no more pain, no more suffering and enjoying her new life with her Lord.

I sensed the sweet fragrance of God and His peace at the funeral and the reception. I believed that God was honouring Eleanore for the way she lived. She honoured God until her death. She served God until the last moment of her life. She kept her faith until the last. Janette and her husband drove me home. I thanked them.

After I arrived home I continually thought about Eleanore. If she did not say, "I am a teacher" when I first met her, and if she did not ask me to write an essay every time she visited, my life would be totally different. Through Eleanore's English lessons I received so much comfort, healing, and abundant blessings. I was so honoured to know Eleanore and to receive English lessons from her. I said in my heart, "Goodbye Eleanore. I am so pleased that I met you on earth and also I am so excited that I will see you in Heaven! Thank you for everything you did for me."

The Celebration of My Books

February 27, 2013

One day after my birthday Pastor Faustin visited me with sushi lunch to celebrate my 75th birthday. While we were eating sushi in my living room Pastor Faustin asked me, "Is there any exciting news?"

"Yes, there is," I replied, "I am going to publish my book." I told him that my essays about the Goodness of God were put together in a book. I was so excited to tell him about it. Then he asked me, "Can I tell this good news at the church?"

"No, please don't do that right now. When the books arrive, I'll let you know. Then you can tell the people about my book."

My books came on the 24th of December. One Sunday in January I took one book to the church and presented it to Pastor Faustin and Marina. The following day while I was out Pastor Faustin left a message on my phone. "Hi Akemi. This is Pastor Faustin calling. Thank you so much for your book. You did a beautiful job. I am very proud of you. I would like to celebrate your books and their author at the church one Sunday. What do you think about it? Let me know. Call me on my cell phone."

But I did not call him because I did not know what to do. Pastor Faustin called me again in the evening. "Akemi, did you get my message? What do you think?" I replied, "I did not call you because I did not know what to do."

"Let's celebrate your books one Sunday."

"Thank you very much, but don't do anything too big, because I can't take it."

Pastor Faustin set the date on the 3rd of February, and told me to prepare a short speech. He also asked Christine Lobo to introduce my books and me on the screen. Christine visited me one evening to see my photos and picked some from my album.

I spoke about the celebration of my book to my trustee, Janis Flowers, my good friend Rita Gervais, and my creative writing class teacher, Anthazia Kadir. Rita was working on that Sunday so she could not come, and Anthazia wanted to attend but she got sick so could not come. Janis agreed to come and celebrate the day with me.

Unfortunately, I had a cold a week before this important day. I suffered from fever and coughing. I was so tired that I could not do anything. I could not prepare even a short speech for my book celebration. One day Christine called me and told me that the celebration would start at 12:30 right after the service. Christine's presentation would be first and my speech to follow. I really thanked her for all she was doing for me.

The night before, lying on my bed I wanted to prepare a short speech for my book celebration, but I could not think straight. I did not want to go to the church the following morning. I just wanted to rest. Then suddenly a good idea came to my mind which is that I simply say a very short speech like "That's the story about my books and me. Christine explained so well that I have nothing more to add. I am very thankful to God for all He did for me." I felt a little ease and fell asleep soon.

Early Sunday morning I drove to the church with 20 new books. Soon Pastor Faustin arrived and set up a table and placed a tablecloth on it for my book. I put my small white tablecloth on top of it and arranged the books tastefully. I attended the intercessors prayer and the service started. Janis Flowers came, and we sat together. We had beautiful worship music and the guest speaker's teaching followed.

When the service ended Pastor Faustin stood up and said to the congregation, "Everyone please take your seats. Akemi published her books. We are going to celebrate her books and the author. Akemi come up here. We are going to celebrate her books with Christine's presentation." I went to the front. Pastor Faustin congratulated me, and I thanked him. When I wanted to go back to my seat he said, "You stay here and we watch the presentation together." I sat in the front row. Then everyone looked at the white screen. The presentation of *Akemi's Journals* was supposed to start. The screen lighted, and the first picture of the title came out but it did not move at all. There was some kind of technical difficulty occurring. Then Pastor Faustin said, "Okay, then let Akemi talk."

What I prepared was "Christine did a good job. I have nothing to add to it. I just want to thank God." But it did not work. I screamed in my heat "God Help!" and started speaking. I told the congregation, "Writing a book was my dream since I was 20 years old. I had such a strong desire to write a book but I never told anybody about it. I did not tell my parents and never told even God. But that dream was always in my heart. Then I came to Canada and my language changed.

About 14 years ago I met a wonderful teacher, Mrs. Eleanore Sproule, and started taking English lessons from her. Soon she told me to write one essay every time she came, and I started writing again. I decided to write about the goodness of God in my life, and kept on writing more than 14 years. Last spring I took a creative writing course at Older Adult Centre and met a teacher, Anthazia Kadir. She read my essays and suggested I could publish them. So it just happened. But I am so thankful that God knew my dreams and He fulfilled it after 55 years," and I added "I truly believe no matter how hard our lives are there is always good things in our lives because God is with us, and He loves each one of us so deeply."

Then the screen started showing Christine's presentation. It started with my photos, beautiful music and her narration. There were many flowers from my garden, and even my art works were presented. It was so graceful. She did an excellent job. When the presentation ended, Pastor Faustin read a short piece from my book, and Pastor Marina also read a piece too, and both of them said, "Akemi's books are there. Please get one."

Then Christine brought me a huge bouquet of pink and white roses. I was so shocked. I was standing in awe, and people started coming to greet me one after another and gave me big hugs and spoke kind words. I was totally overwhelmed. I could not believe it. Soon many people came to the book table and obtained my books.

I autographed each one of the books. It was totally amazing. I never expected these things would happen in my life. It was almost like I was living in a beautiful dream.

That night I really thanked God. Of course, God is God, He knows everything about my life, yet still it was hard to comprehend that He knew my secret dream of writing a book and fulfilled it. I gave thanks again and again to my God who created Heaven and Earth, yet He was concerned about my little dream. I sensed such sweet love from God.

I had a very hard time going to sleep, my mind was so excited and also my spirit was very excited! I could not sleep for a long time, but it was a wonderful day. I will remember this day as long as I live.

Origami Cranes

March 20, 2013

Our art group had a meeting on the 24th of February to plan how we could participate in the coming Family Fun Day at our church. The Family Fun Day was planned to invite the people from our neighbourhood and give them a fun day. Our group leader, Mila, had told us to bring some ideas to the meeting. I wanted to bring some ideas about crafts for children, but could not think about anything at all. I was so disappointed! Out of desperation I made two origami cranes. I know they did not help anything, but it's better than nothing. When I was a little girl my mother taught me how to fold origami. I made so many things like a boat, a kimono, a hat, a rabbit, a frog, flowers, etc. But I could not remember any of them any more. I just knew how to make a crane and a balloon. So I made a couple of balloons too.

On the evening of the 24th I put two paper cranes and two paper balloons into my bag, and I added some origami papers which my sister, Sanae, sent me from Japan many years ago. I felt so sad that I was attending the meeting without any idea. I truly wondered if God can use two origami cranes for His purpose or not.

Our art group is a small group of five, Mila, Lina, Christine, Justin, and I, but I just love to be with them and enjoy attending the meetings. When we were talking about the coming Family Fun Day I put my origami cranes and balloons on the table. Then Justin came into the room, and saw the origami cranes. He pulled a chair closer to the table and started making a very complicated origami flower from the origami paper. He was so skillful and neat! He made a beautiful origami flower in a minute. I found out that Justin's parents came from Japan and Justin was born in Canada. His mother taught him origami when he was young. Justin remembered a lot of things which I had forgotten.

Suddenly origami became a big possibility to serve the children.

Justin said, "I have an origami book written in English. I can bring that book." I said, "I will ask my sister to send more origami paper." Justin and I made more cranes to display. The other ladies decided to serve the children by teaching them how to make wool bracelets and three-dimensional paper art works.

The following day I called my sister, Sanae, in Japan and asked her to send me origami papers by the 9th of March. Then she said, "I can't find origami paper around here. I have to go to the centre of the city. I have to ask my husband to take me. Perhaps we can go this weekend. Then I don't think there is enough time for them to arrive in Mississauga. I am very sorry but I can't do that."

Mail takes at least 7 to 12 days to arrive here from Hiroshima, Japan. I was very disappointed but what could do? I knew I could find origami paper at a Japanese store in Toronto, but I did not want to drive there by myself. I called Michael's, an art and craft store in Meadowvale, and asked, "Do you have origami paper?" "Yes we do." a lady answered. "Do you? Thank you. I will be there soon." When I drove to Michael's I found only one package of origami paper on a shelf. I picked up the package and paid for it. It contained 300 origami papers in different bright colours. I was so pleased!

I went home and made some more cranes from the different coloured papers. Everything was ready.

I made 20 colourful origami cranes and I wanted to display them beautifully. I thought they won't look nice on the table nor in a box, but they must fly in the air. I decided to ask Gary to make a stand for the cranes with a branch nailed on a wooden board. I made a simple sketch of a branch stand and gave it to Gary when he visited me. I also asked him to make it before the 9th of March. He said "Okay I got it."

A few days later I received a parcel from Sanae unexpectedly. She sent me a package of origami. When I called her and thanked her, she was shocked. "Has it arrived already? It took only three days. That's wonderful. I found only one package of origami in the corner of the grocery store where I go. That's good. Thank you for your call." I thanked my sister and also God that everything was working wonderfully well.

On the evening of the 9th of March, Gary brought a huge stand for me. I expected about a 50 cms high stand, but he made it almost one metre high branch stand, and a big brick with a hole in the centre to support the branch. It was definitely much better than I had expected. It was beautiful! I hung some cranes on the branches and showed it to Gary. I thanked him.

On the Family Fun Day, I drove to the church with 20 cranes and the stand. I also took 20 paper balloons in a plastic bowl. As soon as I arrived at the church I put the branch stand on the craft table and hung the cranes. They were so gorgeous, and I was so happy! I prayed in my heart to God to invite many children to the Family Fun Day.

The Sunday service started, and we started worshipping God. I searched for Justin in the room but could not find him. I could not find him for a long time and started worrying about our origami table. "Lord bring Justin here quickly," I asked God in my heart and continued worshipping God. In the middle of the service I saw Justin and thanked God.

The service was very short. By 12 noon all the chairs were removed from the room in preparation for the Family Fun Day. Justin and I sat close to the wall and placed five chairs at the other side of the table. Origami papers and an origami book were on the table.

Soon people started coming to enjoy the fun and to participate in many activities. Many children sat on the chairs to make origami. Justin was a good teacher. He taught the children how to make origami step-by-step, and I helped the children when they could not understand. When one group finished, another group came. So many children enjoyed making origami, and made so many penguins, cranes, treasure boxes, balloons, etc. When the children wanted to make paper balloons Justin said, "That's Akemi's specialty. She will teach you." So I taught them how to make balloons. Justin was a good teacher, and he was so patient with the children. I was so blessed to work with him!

We were so busy from 12 to 4 o'clock, as so many people came to the Family Fun Day. I learned that more than 100 people came that afternoon. We closed the table, and when I got home it was already 4:30 p.m. I was very exhausted but felt so good because we were able to contribute to the Family Fun Day. I asked God to reach out to these children continually, and one day they will come to know Him as their saviour just like He did for me.

I Received a Wonderful Ministry

May 25, 2013

One morning in the early spring I had a strange dream and woke up full of anger. In my dream, I opened my closet and found out all my clothes were gone. I had nothing to wear. Then I found out my cousin, Tsukaho, took all my clothes and put them into garbage bags. I checked the outside, but all the garbage bags were already gone. I was furious and asked Tsukaho, "Why did you throw out all my clothes? I have nothing to wear."

"Because my sister, Mizuko, told me to do so," she replied.

I found Mizuko, Tsukaho's eldest sister and asked her the same question. "Why did you throw out all my clothes? You have no right to do that." Then she said, "But you are living in my house."

My anger increased and I woke up full of anger. It was an awful feeling. I said to God in my bed. "Lord, what is it?" Then soon I realized that I had to cut ungodly soul ties between my cousins and me, so I did. I also realized that I had never cut the soul tie between my grandfather and me, so I did. Then the anger went away very quickly and peace occupied my heart. "This is good. Thank you, Father," I said.

It was truly a strange dream, and I thought about it a lot. I sensed that the enemy has legal right to torment my life. Since my grandfather was a priest of Shintoism I asked for forgiveness on behalf of my ancestors and cut ungodly soul ties, but I wasn't sure if I was free from it or not. I decided to ask for help from our church. Our church is offering Restoring the Foundation Issue Focused Ministry, and there are two couples helping members.

The next Sunday I saw Oscar Ibagon at our Church and said to him, "Good morning Oscar. I would like to take your ministry."

"Oh really? Okay. I will give you the questionnaire. You will answer all the questions and return it to me. Maria will talk to you one day and we will minister to you," he said.

"That's really good. Thank you. I look forward to it."

The following Sunday, Oscar gave me the questionnaire. I took it home. After lunch, I prayed about it and wrote my answers on nine pages. I returned the papers to Oscar the next Sunday.

I wanted to experience total freedom which the Lord Jesus completed on the cross for me without the enemy's interference. The freedom the Lord Jesus gave to me was so great and I haven't experienced it yet. I was so excited about receiving a ministry from Oscar and Maria. But they did not contact me for a long time.

Finally, one Sunday after the service I asked Oscar, "Oscar, you haven't forgotten me, have you?"

"No, no. We are finishing one lady this Friday. After that Maria will call you."

"Thank you. That's good. I am so excited about it."

Maria visited me in the morning of the 16th of May. We admired the beautiful flower garden while sitting on the living room sofas. Maria asked me so many questions about my life, and I answered them, but I had a very comfortable time with her. At the end of our session Maria said, "I will pick you up tomorrow evening and we will minister to you at our apartment."

"At your place, tomorrow?" I asked.

"Yes, tomorrow. Our place is better because we have two sons. We will fast breakfast and lunch, because when we fast we can hear from God clearly. Can you fast?"

"I take pills in the morning so I would like to eat breakfast. I can fast lunch." I replied.

"Can you fast water colour painting?"

"Yes, I can."

"Good, I will come at 5:30 and take you home and we will eat dinner together."

"Dinner with you? Oh this is wonderful. Thank you so much." I could not believe their kindness. I really thanked God for everything He was providing for me.

The following day I fasted lunch and water colour painting. I also did not listen to classical music at all.

At 5:30 exactly, Maria came to pick me up and we drove to the east end of Mississauga. When we arrived at her apartment Oscar was playing soccer with his two sons at the playground. Maria and I went to their apartment and watched soccer from the balcony for a while. Soon I talked to their sons, Santiago and Efraim. They are very intelligent and well-mannered young boys with such huge hopes for their future. I thoroughly enjoyed being with them.

After we had a delicious supper, Oscar and Maria ministered to me. We used the text book. I went through so many issues by forgiveness and self-forgiveness. I dealt with all my issues one after another. I was so thankful and also excited about what I had accomplished. I thanked them. Then Oscar said, "It's not over. This is the exciting part. We will ask God what He is saying to you about your problem. We will ask Him to show you a picture. Let's pray." and he prayed.

I was in trouble because I don't receive pictures from the Lord easily. I said to God in my heart. "Help! I need Your help! Otherwise I don't know what to do."

"Do you see anything?" Maria asked me.

"No, I don't see anything," I answered.

Then suddenly I felt I was in a kitchen. I said, "I am in a kitchen." Then I knew I was in the kitchen of the principal's home. My father was a principal of the elementary school, and the house was built at the edge of the school yard.

"Do you see anybody? What are they doing?" Maria asked me.

"I don't see anybody," I said. "Just a moment. I am going out to the school yard. I am walking through the school yard to the very end. There is a big cave, like a big tunnel. I am in there." When I was in grade two, right before the World War II ended, we had an air raid, and all the students in our class evacuated to the cave. I don't remember how long we were there. When the air raid ended the teacher escorted all the students to the outside. But she said to me, "Akemi you stay here. I will tell your mother to pick you up." Everybody left. I stayed in the cave by myself, but nobody came. It was very dark and lonely. I don't remember how I got out of there."

"Can you forgive your teacher?"

"Yes, I forgive her."

"Can you forgive your mother?"

"Yes, I forgive my mother."

Then they prayed over me.

"Now, let's invite Jesus in this picture. What is He doing?"

"He is in the cave with me. He is sitting and I am on His lap."

"Good Akemi. Well done!" Oscar screamed. They prayed over me and blessed me. It was an awesome experience, and it was truly a wonderful ministry. Oscar drove me home. I thanked God for what He has done from the bottom of my heart. I am free-er than before.

The spring of 2013 started in a wonderful way. It is very exciting to live my life with the Lord!

I Needed Lots of Prayers

June 18, 2013

I have just finished the water colour course at Visual Arts Mississauga last Monday on the 7th of June. It started on the second week of April. I attended every Monday afternoon for 10 weeks. This time I took an advanced course. The reason I took it was that it was an afternoon course. I did not want to drive in the rush hour anymore. It was so hectic, cars were running so slowly, and it took a long time to get to the art class. Since I had been painting water colours for about 10 years I wanted more of a challenge.

The first day I attended the class I knew seven people among the fifteen, and felt very comfortable, and I also knew our teacher Sherell Girard. I truly enjoyed painting with other artists, and it was so wonderful to go out once a week. Attending the art classes was like my holiday. However, this time was different. I faced lots of challenges and I needed lots of prayers.

Sherell did not want us to use too much pencil drawing. That was a big challenge for me. She also did not give us the complete picture to paint. We had to compose the whole picture from a little bit of information and to use our imagination. That was a big stretch for me. The first day started with negative painting. The whole picture was done by negative painting. When we complained, Sherell said, "You took an advanced course right?" We all laughed, but I really needed prayers.

One time we painted a rusted bucket and an old barn. They were not my desirable objects to paint. That day while I was driving to the class I really prayed to God. "Lord help me. I really don't like to paint a rusted bucket and an old barn. Please help me. Make me enjoy painting a rusted bucket and an old barn. I really need your help." At the class Sherell gave us an enlarged photo of a rusted bucket and an old barn, so it was much easier to paint, and surprisingly I enjoyed painting rust and deteriorated wood. I used a dry brush to paint the old wood. Unexpectedly it turned out to be a good painting. I really thanked God for His help.

One day we painted apple blossoms by pouring colour instead of using a brush. It was my first experience of pouring colour on the paper. We needed small plastic containers to make coloured water. We made different coloured water in the different containers and poured them on the paper. My apple blossoms did not turn out to be very beautiful. I wanted to do it again at home, but I did not have time to do it. I finished the background, branches, and leaves. I completed it, but I still did not like it at all. It wasn't a successful experience at all.

I cried to God in my heart, "Oh God, oh God. What shall I do? Help me!" I may try it again at home one day. While I was struggling Sherell came to see my work. I asked her, "How can I improve this painting? Should I darken the background?" Then she said, "No, no, don't touch it. Just add your signature. That's it. Good job."

One day we went out and painted whatever we wanted. It was a very good exercise, and I enjoyed it very much. I painted a part of the park behind our art buildings, blue sky, lots of green trees, two red chestnut trees, and green grass. I enjoyed it very much, the freedom to paint, the beautiful nature which God created. I enjoyed every moment of painting and finished it very quickly. That was a wonderful experience and I thanked God for that.

On the 3rd of June, we painted the whole painting by pouring colour. A week before Sherell told us about pouring colour and what to prepare, but I did not understand at all. I prepared some small plastic containers, many tubes of different colours, and a big apron.

When I arrived at the class, Sherell had already displayed some pictures which were done by pouring colours. When I saw them I was totally shocked. The pictures were done by masking fluid and pouring colours. They were nicely done, but I did not have any control over the art work. It was very scary. Sherell suggested that we paint a landscape or an abstract. I decided to paint an abstract. The abstract painting was done with striking red colour and light yellow and violet. The bottom 2/3 was pure red and the top 1/3 was yellow and violet. It was quite nice, and I wished to paint that. It was my first abstract painting, because I had never painted abstract.

Before I started drawing with masking fluid, I took time and prayed to God. "Lord help me! I am going to paint my first abstract painting with striking red colour. I really want to paint something beautiful. I don't want to paint a hell or slaughter house. It has to be graceful, something like a part of Heaven. Help!" Then I started drawing many lines on the paper with masking fluid. While the masking fluid was drying I made three pouring colours in the little plastic containers, red, light yellow and violet. I put on an apron, and placed a big towel on the table, and a big container lid on the towel to catch the colour. I poured red colour on the paper first. While I was moving the paper Sherell came to help me. She said, "You need more red."

"I did not make any more," I replied. Then she went to her table and made red coloured liquid and brought it to me. She said, "Add this." I replied: "Thank you. You are so kind."

I poured more red over the paper and held the paper quite a long time until it stopped dripping. Then I dried it with a hair dryer thoroughly. Then I poured light yellow and violet on the top side. This time I used a water spray to control colour and shape. That's all I did and dried it. When the paper was completely dried I removed the masking fluid and painted with light yellow over the white line. I took the lid to the sink and emptied and washed it.

I truly hoped that I did not paint hell, but it turned out to be quite a peaceful abstract. Even though lots of red colour was used, it wasn't hell. It was fire in heaven. I was so pleased. The light yellow and light violet moving upward like the glory of God going up, and the fire of God coming down. I was so pleased and thanked God from the bottom of my heart. "Thank you, Father, I painted my first abstract. It is so peaceful and even glorious. Thank you so much for Your help. I could not have done it by myself."

I titled the painting "Catch the Fire" the name of our church.

I am so thankful to God for the way I spent the last 10 weeks.

Restored Garden

August 15, 2013

The flower garden in my backyard was so beautiful in the year 2000, the year my husband, Ken, passed away. The garden was full of flowers and they kept on blooming all that summer. I took so many photos to remember my husband's favourite garden. It was a truly beautiful and colourful garden! Since then the garden changed little by little every year. The perennials came out every spring, but they did not bloom as they used to, and some disappeared gradually. My neighbour's ash tree which was planted very close to the fence grew more and more every year and started covering the garden. The left side of the garden became so shady, that some flowers stopped blooming completely. I moved some flowers from the left to the right to save them.

One summer we had a water shortage and the city of Mississauga banned watering the lawn. I had a very hard time to look after the garden. It was so painful to watch flowers dying from the lack of water. My heart ached to watch them.

I found so many problems in looking after the garden. One summer rabbits invaded the garden, and ate lots of the stems of the flowers and damaged the garden so badly. I tried so many ways to stop the rabbits' invasion, but nothing worked. Finally, my good friend Diego put chicken wire all around the yard at the bottom of the wire fence.

Every year I enjoyed the garden. The presence of the Lord is so strong and I had such peace in the garden. Every time I watered the double rainbows appeared, and they made me so happy. The garden is my sanctuary. I could not think about my life without the garden. But every year fewer flowers bloomed. The last two years the flowers did not bloom much on the left side of the garden. Many buds were formed, but they did not open at all, and I had a hard time watching them. "Lord, Your garden is not blooming nicely. I am so sorry. I am trying my best. Lord, look at these buds, they never even opened." I said to God in the sad garden.

Then last fall I asked Jerry, who built the new deck and fence, to cut the tall apple tree from the corner of my backyard. Also Diego came with a brand new electric saw and cut off the big branch from my neighbour's ash tree. Diego said, "Don't worry Akemi. It's okay to cut the branches in your property," and he added, "you will have a beautiful flower garden next year." I really felt bad to cut my neighbour's branch, but I really thanked Diego for his kind act.

This year, the year 2013, the garden was so beautiful. We had many rainy days from the late spring to the early summer. Rain came so steadily that I did not have to water the garden at all until August. I truly thanked God for that. I just fertilized the garden regularly. The perennials grew so healthily and started blooming beautifully.

Spring flowers bloomed; lady's mantle, bleeding heart, columbine, balloon flowers, and they lasted so long. Soon early summer flowers added the colour in the garden, like clematis, Maltese Cross, spiderwort, meadow sweet, daylily. The garden was full of different colours, yellow, pink, white, red, blue and purple. It was so glorious! I enjoyed every moment of the garden. I spent lots of time in the garden and said to Him, "Lord, Your garden is so beautiful this year. I never had such a beautiful garden for the last 13 years. Thank you so much for wonderful rain and the sunshine."

It's already August, yet the flowers are blooming beautifully. Summer flowers added more colours in the garden, like Shasta daisy, cone flowers, small sunflowers, glove thistle. It reminded me of the garden of the year 2000. I am so pleased and enjoyed being in the garden.

I invited many friends this year and spent blessed time with them. On the 11th of July, Rita and I invited Norma and prayed over her and blessed her. Norma enjoyed the fellowship and also the garden. I thanked God for the wonderful afternoon we spent in the garden, and also His deep love for each one of His children.

On the 25th of July, I invited Marlene Traas. Rita joined us and she drove to Oakville to pick up Marlene. We had lunch in the living room looking at the garden in full bloom. We had a truly wonderful time with one another and with God. He blessed us so much that we prayed for each other for our blessed future with God. I was so pleased that God joined us and enjoyed us. It was an awesome summer day, and I really thanked God for the precious time He gave us!

One evening in August, Susanne Chung called me suddenly and asked me about my garden, so I invited her to see the garden. Then in the evening of the 5th of August Susanne and her husband Jeffrey, and her mother, visited me. I showed them the garden, and offered summer fruits. We spent a beautiful summer evening together. It was so wonderful and also a blessing.

The garden is in full bloom this year, even on the left side of the garden every bud opened. Lots of water and enough light made every flower bloom. I was so thrilled and very thankful for that.

Gary came and cut the grass regularly. He did a neat job in the garden as usual. The first day he came into my life he said, "I am your gardener," and made me cry. He is still a wonderful gardener and a precious friend. I am thoroughly enjoying the beautiful garden of the summer of the year 2013!

From the Prayer Meeting

September 2, 2013

One cool evening of August the 12th, Rita and I attended Young Wha's prayer meeting. When we arrived, there were already 13 people in her basement and they were talking to one another. Young Wha gave so many good reports with such excitement. In her report, she mentioned that her good friend in Hokkaido Japan was visiting Laos and Cambodia now. Then she started talking about how bad the Japanese were in Asian countries during the war and how the Japanese soldiers treated the people over there. She added that her mother still remembers so clearly the ordeal her country's people went through. After some more reports she realized that I was in the group, and said, "Oh, Akemi is here. I forgot about it. I am sorry."

I said, "We did very bad things that's true," and asked everyone there, "May I have some time to ask forgiveness to God for what we did?" They said yes to me.

This wasn't the first time I heard what the Japanese people did during the war. When I came to Canada in 1970, and started attending George Brown College to study English as a second language, a young Korean man approached me and asked me, "Are you a Japanese?" When I said, "Yes, I am." he said with anger, "Why did your people occupy Korea? Why did they do all the bad things to our people? Why? I would like to know the answer." I sensed his enormous anger, but did not know any answers to his questions.

I knew Japan occupied Korea, China, and other Asian countries during the war, but did not have any knowledge about what we did, because I was so little and also the bad things we did in other countries were not written in our history books. I remember so clearly that moment! I could not even look at his face and said with a very small voice, "We are sorry for what we did to your people. Please forgive us. I am so sorry." That was all I could say. But he left me. That day I realized that I was not living in Japan any more, and felt so sad even after I said sorry. It was 43 years ago.

After I got permission from everybody I prayed for forgiveness from God for what we did in the Asian countries and how we treated the people so badly. I asked God to forgive us and cleanse us from our sins. I also asked God to give us a new start. I welcomed the Holy Spirit to Japan to save the Japanese people. The tears started coming down from my eyes. When I finished my prayers, a man said immediately, "Your sins are forgiven," and he blessed Japan and our future. Then Marry, a Korean lady, said, "I am a Korean and my mother really hates Japanese people, but I forgive you. I forgive everything you did to us." I said, "Thank you."

Our prayer meeting went on. When I said 43 years ago "I am sorry" to a young Korean man I felt so sad and wanted to cry, but this time was different. I felt so relieved and had peace in my heart. I thanked God in my heart that He gave me this wonderful opportunity to confess the sins of Japan. Soon I started yawning. I yawned and yawned as if I was experiencing a deliverance. I enjoyed the prayer meeting and worshiped God with my brothers and sisters in the Lord.

A few days later I received a call from Carol Hay. She said that her friend, Evelyn Martinez was in Japan now to pray and worship in Japan. She also asked me to pray for Evelyn. I was so thrilled and also thanked God for sending wonderful intercessors to Japan. God never forgets us. He wants to save Japanese people more than I desire. I thanked God from the bottom of my heart and asked His blessing and protection over Evelyn and her group in Japan.

When I met Rita the next time she said, "Akemi I have to tell you that Young Wha sent me an email, and it said that Glenn, a man in our prayer meeting saw a picture of the Japanese map while you were praying for Japan. The Japanese map was green and busy, but when you prayed and asked for forgiveness for Japan it became white. Isn't that nice?"

"Yes, it is. Thank you for telling me."

I was so thrilled to know that even my little prayer contributes to the future of Japan. I could not grasp the reality of the spiritual world. I felt so thankful that God can use even my little prayers.

Only a few days later Carol called me and read an email from Evelyn. In her email, she said that her group climbed up Mt. Fuji, the most famous mountain in Japan and did spiritual war fare. She said, "The enemy is defeated." While I was listening to Carol's message my body started tingling from head to toe. I said, "Thank you so much Carol. I am so pleased. God never forgets us. He wants to save us." Then Carol said "Amen" on the phone. I truly thanked God for His love and desire to save the Japanese people. I really hope that the Japanese people will receive Jesus as their saviour very soon. I want them to live full lives knowing their loving Father.

Violets from Carol

June 30, 2003

He Gave Me His Best

September 29, 2013

One day in early September while I was ironing my blouse steam started gushing out from the iron and did not stop. I shut off the iron and knew that I could not use the iron any more. Was it the time to get a new one? I used this iron for 13 years. I still remember so clearly that this iron was the first thing I bought by myself after my husband's death. 13 years was a long time. This was the time to say good-bye.

I went to Canadian Tire and found the same make of iron and obtained it. I did not know why, but the cashier deducted an extra 10 dollars from the cost of 39 dollars. So I bought a very nice iron for only 29 dollars. I thought it was a good deal, and drove home with thanksgiving in my heart. "Thank you, Father, I got a brand new iron so cheaply. It's unbelievable! Thank you so much." I came home and finished ironing my blouse.

Only a few days later while I was altering my friend Carol's pants, my sewing machine did not start at all. I tried to press the speed controller with my right foot in so many different angles and realized that the sewing machine ran when I pressed the left side of the speed controller very gently. I used the sewing machine very slowly and patiently. Finally, I finished the pants and started making a cushion cover, but the sewing machine started running so fast and would not stop at all. I was so scared, I turned off the switch, and thought that this is it. I can't use this sewing machine any more.

I still had a few items to alter, I put my right hand over the sewing machine and blessed it. Somehow, I was able to use the sewing machine again, and I finished all Carol's clothes. But the sound was so loud that I knew I could not use it any more.

I called the Singer store in Shoppers World and talked to a lady. When I mentioned my problem about my sewing machine she said, "I think you need a new speed controller. Bring over your speed controller. I will give you a new one." I thanked her but I knew it wasn't only a problem of the speed controller, but also the sewing machine. Could I fix it or is it time to buy a new one? I thought in my mind, I have been using this sewing machine for more than 40 years. I felt so comfortable using it. If I buy a new one I will have to buy a table too. So many thoughts came to my mind, but one thing I knew was that I needed a sewing machine.

The following morning after I cleaned the garden I entered the living room and wanted to listen to classical music, but the stereo did not work, and only a strange sound came out from it. I pressed different buttons to change the stations but none of them worked. I found out that I could use a tape but not a CD. Could I fix it or is it time to buy a new one? I was so upset.

I took a small portable radio from the basement and put it on the stereo set, and listened to music, but the sound wasn't so good.

About 20 years ago while my husband was still working at Atomic Energy of Canada Limited, he took a course to quit smoking, and successfully quit smoking. At that time, his instructor suggested to him to buy something nice to celebrate his success, and he bought a very nice stereo set. It's a part of my living room furniture with lots of memories attached to it.

I thought to myself that maybe it was time to say goodbye to old things and buy new ones, a new sewing machine and a new stereo set. It's nice but it is costly! I was so confused about what to do and also so frustrated. That night I talked to God and said, "Father, as you know I am in trouble. My sewing machine is not working and my stereo set is broken. I really don't know what to do, to buy new ones or fix them. I am confused. I put this situation into your hands. Father give me Your best for this situation. Thank you."

Every time I used the sewing machine I thought that I had to do something about it, and then said to myself, "Akemi, don't worry about it. It's already in God's hand. Just be patient and wait," and the peace of God came to me.

One day when Gary came to cut the grass I mentioned about my sewing machine. Then he said, "I will take you to the Singer store. I will have a week off next week and after I go to my aunt's cottage I will take you."

"Really? Thank you. If you take me I would like to take my sewing machine and ask if it is worth fixing or if I need to buy a new one."

"Okay. Let's do it."

A few days later Gary drove me to Shopper's World and he carried my sewing machine to the Singer store. He put the sewing machine on the table in the store. The owner of the store was so excited when he saw my old sewing machine. "Oh, this is the original Stylist. It's over 40 years, right?"

"Yes, it is. My question is, is it worth fixing it or is it time to buy a new one?"

He replied immediately. "This was a very expensive sewing machine. You paid 500 dollars 40 years ago. I will fix it for you, and you can use it for another 40 years.

"Really?"

"Yes, it is a good one. You need a new speed controller. I will fix it for you and call you in a couple of days."

I was so relieved and said thank you to the man and also to God.

This summer Gary's co-worker Debbie asked me to do alterations for her dresses and her daughter's dress, so I did. Then she asked me to paint a landscape with her son and his fiancé in it as her wedding gift for her son, so I painted it. I also went to De Serres, an art supply store, with her to frame it. Debbie was very pleased with my work. One evening she brought a thank you card and money for my painting and a gift card. I was stunned by her kindness and offered her a cup of tea in my living room. While I was talking I just mentioned about my broken stereo set. Then Debbie said, "My brother is an electrical technician. I am sure he can fix it for you."

"Really?" I was totally shocked, "Can he fix it for me?"

"Of course. That's his job. I will bring him here and let him see your stereo set."

"Thank you so much. That's wonderful." I almost screamed.

A couple of days later Debbie came with her brother, and in a short time he fixed my stereo set so wonderfully. It sounded better than before. I was so happy. I thanked them again and again. I did not have to take my stereo set to the repair shop and I did not have to buy a new one. It was so wonderful.

When I received a call from the Singer store, Gary drove me again to the store and we took my sewing machine home. Gary put it back on the sewing table. When I stepped on the new speed controller it ran so smoothly. I was so pleased and happy.

I thanked God from the bottom of my heart. "Thank you, Father, You truly gave me Your best. My sewing machine runs like new, and my stereo set sounds better than before. I did not have to spend any money for it. You took care of me so wonderfully! I am so grateful that I am your daughter! Thank you so much."

The Two Letters from Japan

November 30, 2013

I received an unexpected letter from Katsuko Kiso in Japan. She introduced herself as a member of the Mihara Lutheran Church where I was baptized 48 years ago. She wrote that at the Lutheran Church the ladies' group was using my book, *Akemi's Journals* for their meetings. Pastor Tanigawa was translating word-to-word in Japanese. She asked me if I had a Japanese version of my book. She also said that if I didn't have a Japanese version she wanted to have an English book, because the book they were using at their meeting belonged to Mrs. Urano. Mrs. Urano is my good friend. Once she visited Canada, and my husband, Ken, and I took her to Niagara Falls. When I visited Japan last time, I stayed at her house for a few days, and she and her husband treated me so kindly. Since she is a retired English teacher I sent one book to her last Easter as a gift.

When I learned that the ladies at the Mihara Lutheran Church were using my book for their meetings, I was surprised. I never thought about it or imagined it. It was a totally unexpected surprise.

Unfortunately, I didn't have a Japanese version so I sent her an English one. I thought about translating my book to Japanese by myself, but it was so much work. I realized that I could not handle it.

After I sent Katsuko my book nothing happened for a long time. From time to time I wondered if my book had arrived there or not.

After two months, I received another letter from Katsuko. She received my book and thanked me. She included many photos of the members of the Mihara Lutheran Church. Katsuko wrote that she is planning to have a celebration to commemorate 14 years of her husband's death in June 2014, and wants to give my books to her friends who helped her. She already asked Pastor Tanigawa to translate my book and he agreed to do that. She asked my permission to publish the Japanese version of my book in Japan.

It was truly another shocking letter. Somebody wants to spend money to publish my books. It was wonderful, but I felt very uncomfortable in my heart, like somebody is touching my baby, changing her clothes or hair style. I wanted to say, "Don't touch my baby. Leave her alone." I struggled to write a letter to Katsuko for a few weeks.

One evening my good friend Rita visited me and we prayed together. I asked Rita about Katsuko's request to publish the Japanese version of my book and also I told her my feelings about that. Rita said to me, "Akemi, these books are not yours any more. They are God's."

What a wise answer! If my Japanese books bring glory to God, I had to do that. Yet I could not write a letter. One evening I called Bill Dupley, our home group leader, and asked him for his opinion about the Japanese translation of my book. He said immediately, "That's wonderful Akemi. Let them do it. It's so good that more people will read about the goodness of God. All right?" He explained to me so many things. Bill also published his book, *The Secret Place* before, and already it is translated into four different languages. I was so glad I talked to him!

After I talked to Bill, I decided to go ahead with my Japanese books. I thought that if Pastor Tanigawa will translate my books, his Japanese is much better than mine. I don't have to worry about it. I wrote a letter to Katsuko giving her my permission to publish the Japanese version of my book, and thanked her. I prayed asking God to bless Pastor Tanigawa when he translates my book.

I have lots of wonderful memories at the Mihara Lutheran Church. At that church, I heard about Jesus for the first time in my life. I did not know anything about God's love, but the people accepted me as a member of the family, and taught me and helped me to go through my life. I was baptized at that church and became a child of God. God took me into His family. That was the best thing that has happened in my entire life. The people in the church were so kind to me.

On the day I left Mihara to come to Canada, Pastor Asami and many members of the church came to the Mihara train station to say goodbye to me. They came to the platform in the station and sang hymns for me to bless my new journey into a different country.

Since I came to Canada I could not contact them. I truly regret it, but now the ladies in the church were reading my book, and my Japanese book will be published. I hope and pray that even one person could come to know God's deep love for him or her from my Japanese book.

Katsuko promised to send one copy of the Japanese version of *Akemi's Journals* to me when the books are published. I am very excited about it, and thanked God for that.

The Year 2014 Started

January 28, 2014

The year 2014 started with a cold spell. The cold weather lasted for long, day after day, week after week the temperature was minus 15°C to minus 25°C. I felt just like I was living in a freezer. I did not attend Young Wah's prayer meeting on the first Monday of January. That night the temperature was -45°C. I just stayed home. But for some reason I was so excited to be living in the year 2014. The spirit in me was so excited and I felt it. I often wondered why?

One cold evening my good friend, Rita, called me. "Akemi, are you free tonight?"

"Yes, I am. As a matter of fact, I just finished supper."

"I haven't eaten supper yet, but I would like to come and pray with you."

"Okay, that's nice." I said, but I was amazed about Rita. She wanted to come out on this cold night. I washed the dishes, and prepared my living room for our first prayer meeting of 2014, asking God for His blessing over us.

Around eight o'clock Rita came. We chatted for a while over a cup of tea, and our conversation changed to prayers. We thanked God for His unfailing love for us year after year. My heart was filled with thanksgiving towards God and His love. I opened my Bible and read Ephesians 3:16-19:

I pray that out of His glorious riches He may strengthen you with power through His spirit in your inner being, so that Christ may dwell in your heart through faith. And I pray that you, being rooted and established in love, may have power, together with all the saints, to group how wide and long and high and deep is the love of Christ, and to know the love that surpasses knowledge, that you may be filled to the measure of all the fullness of God.

Then Rita said, "I saw the thick and heavy door has just closed tightly." The Lord was giving Rita a vision.

"What does that mean?" I asked.

"You know the special door like the safety room in a bank where they keep money. We are so safe now. Nobody can come in," she replied.

"Alright. Nobody can steal the love of God from us." I thought in my mind. Then suddenly my palms started tingling as if the fire of God was touching my palms. I don't usually talk about what my body is feeling, but this time it did not go away for a long time. My palms tingled and tingled so I said, "You know Rita, my palms are tingling so much now." Then Rita opened her eyes and looked at me and said, "Do you know why? Do you know why?"

"No, I don't. I have no clue."

"Because God is giving us a new sword."

Then I knew the reason for the tingling in my palms. The new sword comes with more responsibility and I must use it wisely. While I was thinking about the new sword, Rita said, "We can cut deception with the new sword. While I was using it the darkness disappeared and light came."

We sat quietly for a long time to receive what God was doing for us. Then Rita said, "I see a cloud of people now."

"Who are they?" I asked.

"They are watching us. Akemi, they are encouraging us. I think they are the cloud of witnesses. You know the Bible says a cloud of witnesses. Where is it?"

"It's Hebrew 12," I said and opened my Bible and read it.

Therefore, since we are surrounded by such a great cloud of witnesses, let us throw off everything that hinders and the sin that so easily entangles, and let us run with perseverance the race marked for us. Let us fix our eyes on Jesus, the author and perfector of our faith, who for the joy set before Him endured the cross, scorning its shame, and sat down at the right hand of the throne of God.

Hebrew 12: 1-2

I felt strongly that God wants us to run the race marked for us, and we are surrounded by a great cloud of witnesses. I was so encouraged.

Rita and I prayed until 10:30 pm. It was so wonderful that God joined our prayers. I truly thanked God that we started the year 2014 with such wonderful prayers.

Even though the weather was severe and lots of snow piled up on the ground, my heart was full of excitement and hope. I sensed that this year would be so special for me. I often wondered in my heart why? Why is this year so special? Then one day while I was sweeping the kitchen floor suddenly the thought came to me that exactly 50 years ago I started seeking God in Japan. That was the year 1964 when I visited a little church in Mihara city for the first time. I stopped sweeping the floor and stood there for a long time. I could not believe that 50 years had passed. I also remembered clearly that the first words God spoke to me through the Bible was Jeremiah 29:11-14.

For I know the plans I have for you," declares the Lord, "plans to prosper you and not harm you, plans to give you hope and a future. Then you will call me and come and pray to me, and I will listen to you. You will seek me and find me when you seek me with all your heart I will be found by you, declares the Lord.

When I read these verses I was literally shocked, and thought that I could find the living God because He says so. I wanted to find God so badly. So many memories went through my mind so quickly, of the 50 years that had passed. It had not been an easy ride. I went through many mountains and valleys, and shed lots of tears, but I found God, the living God as He promised in the Bible. All I could think about was God's faithfulness. He never left me nor forsook me. He carried me through so wonderfully. I simply wanted to live my life without depression. That's all I wanted, but now He calls me His daughter and blesses me with pouring out His love over me.

I started praying to God with the broom still in hand. "Heavenly Father, thank You so much for the last 50 years. It has been awesome to live a life with You. I just wanted to live my life without depression when I started seeking You 50 years ago. I never thought my life would be this good to live with Your blessings. You adopted me as Your daughter. Your precious Son died for me. You give me hope, joy, peace, and true life, and my name is written on the book in Heaven. Oh Father, I never expected this wonderful life! Thank you so much."

While I was praying the tears started falling from my eyes. I had an awesome moment with my Heavenly Father in my kitchen.

The year 2014 started so beautifully! I was so thankful to God, and at the same time so excited to live this year with God's blessings.

A Visitor in the Cold Winter

March 6, 2014

On the 27th of January, I heard a message on my answering machine from Sayomi, my Japanese friend, who lives in New York. She wanted to visit me soon and wanted to discuss her schedule with me. She left her cell phone number. When I called her cell phone, I got a message that I needed to add the long distance number 1 and then the area code. I opened the telephone book to find out the New York area code, but there were so many listed. I simply could not contact her.

That evening I tried one more time to call her without the area code and surprisingly I was able to talk to her. Sayomi said, "I need to fix my tooth so badly, and I contacted Dr. Chow. He said that he will be on vacation from the 10th of February to the 17th. I want to go see him before then."

I said, "You can stay at my home, but the weather is so bad. It's very cold."

"As long as it's not snowing I can take the cold," she said.

"Well a snow storm is coming too."

I really did not go out on cold days, as the temperature was below -20°C. I did not want to even drive a car on those days. Sayomi said, "I will call you tomorrow morning and let you know my plan."

"Okay, I will wait for your call," I said.

The next morning, I waited and waited for Sayomi's call, but she never called me. I started sewing my pants and enjoyed the very quiet day. Then suddenly around 3 o'clock the telephone rang. It was Sayomi. She said, "I have arrived at the Toronto airport now. I could not rent a car, but I will come to you by bus. I will see you soon."

I stopped sewing my pants and made a sofa bed and took out

towels. I prepared the guest room nicely and came down to the living room. I sat on the sofa, and prayed to God. "Father as you know Sayomi is coming soon. I really need Your blessing. I want you to bless her stay here, and give us good weather so that I can drive her to the dentist. I need Your help over this whole situation."

Sayomi arrived shortly after. I was surprised. She said that she took a bus from the airport to Square One, and from Square One to Meadowvale. She said, "It cost me only 3 dollars 25 cents," and she laughed.

It was too cold to go out so I cooked whatever I had in the fridge and we ate a simple supper, and talked a lot. Sayomi said, "You look much healthier and happier than the last time I saw you."

"Thank you, the last tine you saw me I had pain on my back, but I don't have it any more. God healed me wonderfully."

We talked and talked. She just moved from Arizona to New York, and was taking logistics and English at college, and working at a Japanese company during the week and at a nice Japanese restaurant on weekends. She told me about her life in New York.

The following morning, on Wednesday, I drove Sayomi to Dr. Chow and picked her up from the dentist. It was very cold, but it did not snow. I truly thanked God. That afternoon I attended our home group and Sayomi rested at my home.

On Thursday, I drove her to the dentist and picked her up. Her front tooth was removed and she got a new tooth very quickly. She looked very nice. Dr. Chow did a very good job and Sayomi was very happy.

On Saturday, it snowed and snowed all day. Sayomi and I cleaned the driveway many times. I was so glad that Sayomi helped me. We wanted to go to church on Sunday, but I wasn't sure if I could drive my car in the snow or not.

On Sunday morning after we ate breakfast Sayomi and I started clearing the driveway. Even though we had shovelled many times on Saturday about 10 cms of snow now covered the driveway. While

I was taking out the snow blower a white car came by and parked on the driveway in front of my house, and Gary got out. He said to me, "Akemi, you don't have to use the snow blower. I will clear it." and he shovelled my driveway so quickly and even helped with my neighbour's driveway. I introduced Sayomi to him and thanked him. It was done so quickly that Sayomi and I were able to go to church.

At the church, we had a communion together in Japanese. Pastor Faustin prayed over Sayomi, and one lady said that she saw a dark tornado over Sayomi's head and offered a prayer. She prayed, "Don't run before Him. He will direct your path. Wait for Him. He will let you know."

We also attended Young Wah's prayer meeting, and after we prayed for the nations, one lady came to Sayomi and prayed over her. She said, "I saw a picture of you breaking something like clay. I believe you are breaking the deception over Japanese people," and blessed her.

One snowy morning we were able to pray for Japan. We prayed that the Japanese people will come to know their creator, the true God. We broke deceptions and confusions over Japanese people and asked God to open their spiritual eyes and ears to see and hear from the true God. Every time I prayed God showed Sayomi a clear picture of Japanese people changing from death to life, and old skins dropped little by little, and finally the light started shining from Japan. Sayomi was so excited to tell me what God was showing her. We truly thanked God and were so happy that we were able to pray for Japan, where we had come from, and where our families still live.

In the afternoon Rita drove us to a restaurant to celebrate our friend Stephanie's 55th birthday. Rita's car slid many times in the heavy snow, but we had a good time in the restaurant. We truly experienced a Canadian winter.

Since Sayomi's student visa was going to expire in a year, I wondered if I would see her again after she goes back to Japan. I wanted to tell her what I learned from God through my life experience. I told her to never forget to thank God because thanksgiving is the key to the Kingdom of God. Especially since we were both born into families who worship idols and have nothing to do with Christianity. God took us from the darkness to the light. We always have lots to thank Him for. I also emphasized to her to look at God instead of looking at problems, because God is always bigger than any problems we face on the earth. Sayomi really thanked me. I also told her, "If God says to you to visit Mississauga, please come. We will have a blessed time together."

On the 7th of February, after a very early lunch I drove Sayomi to Meadowvale bus station. It was a bitterly cold day, but Sayomi left safely on a GO bus to the airport. While I was driving home by myself thanksgiving bubbled up in my heart to God, and I thanked God again and again for His help. In spite of this cold and snowy weather, I was able to take Sayomi to the dentist three times and our church. Many people prayed over her and I blessed her. We also prayed for Japan, and I felt that something changed in Japan.

A few days later I received a thank you card from Sayomi. She wrote that it was a meaningful trip to Mississauga, and her life was changed by knowing God's deep love for her. She also wrote that she realized how beautiful it is to live a life with God. She also thanked me for the gift of three water colour paintings. I was so pleased and thanked God for everything He did for her.

Teddy bear from Ingrid

Jan 25, 2004

Grocery Shopping with Marilyn

April 30, 2014

I called my friend, Marilyn Wubbenhorst, before Christmas last year, but she wasn't there, so I left a message. About a month later Marilyn called me and told me that she had a minor heart attack and was in the Credit Valley Hospital for a while and now she was staying at her daughter's house. She promised to contact me when she got back to her home. It was a great shock to me because she is much younger than I am. I prayed in my heart for God's healing and a quick recovery for her.

Marilyn and I attended the same church, Meadowvale Community Church, about 35 years ago. I recalled that she played the piano for worship. We attended the Ladies' Bible Study together, and learned of God's love for us. I don't recall when, but she left the church and I left the church some years later. Then I lost my husband and she lost her husband a couple of years later. We did not meet often, but once in a month or two she would call me and say "Are you free this evening? Let's go to Swiss Chalet. I will pick you up at 5:30." She arrived exactly at 5:30. We went to Swiss Chalet and had a good time over our chicken dinner.

About a month later Marilyn called me and said, "I am at home now, but I can't drive a car right now. If you want to go to Swiss Chalet you can pick me up this time."

"Okay, I will do that. Do you need any groceries? If you need anything let me know. I will pick them up for you." I said.

"Oh thanks, but my daughter took me grocery shopping yesterday, and she will come next weekend again, so I am okay."

"If you need anything let me know, alright? Take care."

Since then I called Marilyn and asked her about grocery shopping often, but she said she was okay, so I stopped asking her. Then one day she called me and said, "Akemi, are you going grocery shopping soon? Please take me. I need some groceries."

I drove to Marilyn's house immediately and saw a big "For Sale" sign on her front yard. We went to Longo's to shop. I asked her, "Is it okay to go to Longo's? I always do my shopping there."

"Oh sure it's okay with me," she said. Longo's is not too big a store and parking is very easy for me. Even though the price is a little higher than other big stores, but the fruits and the vegetables are so fresh.

"The price is a little high over there. Is that okay with you?" I asked.

"Of course it's okay, Akemi. When I sell this house lots of money will come in."

"Oh good. I am glad to hear that."

We went to Longo's and Marilyn walked from the parking lot to the store. I offered her a shopping cart and she did her shopping by herself. I picked up a few items for myself. At the cashier Marilyn asked for help from a store worker to carry her goods to my car and put them into the trunk. We drove back to her house. I carried her grocery bags to the kitchen and opened the fridge to put them in. I gasped. The fridge was almost empty. I put some groceries into the fridge and the others into the pantry. I said to her, "Marilyn, if you need anything let me know, okay?"

"Thank you, I will." she said.

"Are you attending your church?" I asked, but she did not say anything.

"You take care and I will call you," I said goodbye to her and drove home.

A week later Marilyn called me and said, "Could you take me to Swiss Chalet today around 5 o'clock?"

"You know I really don't like to drive a car at night," I said.

"No, no, we can come back by 6:30. People are coming to take a look at my house from 5 to 6:30, and I have to be out during this time."

"Okay, then I will pick you up at a quarter to 5."

We went to Swiss Chalet and enjoyed a quarter chicken dinner and each other as we used to do. Marilyn said, "I haven't been here for a long time. I am so glad that we were able to come." I was glad that I joined her. While we were talking Marilyn suddenly said, "You know you asked me if I am attending the church. I am not because I simply can't drive. The Pastor visited me at the hospital and stayed about 30 minutes. That's all. Nobody contacted me since then. I can't drive a car right now and I can't go to the church. That's the way it is."

"I am so sorry." I said, and felt so sad in my heart. I did not have anything to say. After dinner I drove her home, and waited about 10 minutes on her street, because people were still in her house. Right after they left in a blue car I drove my car onto her driveway.

The following day I had sadness in my heart all day as I remembered Marilyn's situation. I did not know what to do about this sadness. In the afternoon, I sat on the sofa in the living room and started talking to God about Marilyn's situation. Then the sadness increased to the point I wanted to cry. I said to God. "Lord, we are sorry, forgive us. We are supposed to love one another as You do to us, but we are not doing it. We are hurting one another. Father forgive us. Nobody takes Marilyn to her church and her fridge was empty. We are so sorry. Please forgive us." I cried to God and cried to myself, and felt the sadness of God in my heart so deeply.

He gave His son to die on the cross to save us, and He put His love into our hearts by the Holy Spirit so that we can love one another. Yet, we are not exercising His love toward each other, instead we are hurting one another. I said to God many times we are sorry, but the sadness did not leave all day. At night in my bed I said to God in my heart, "Lord I feel so sad about what's going on in the body of Christ. I am really sorry. But Father I can't live with this deep sorrow in my heart. Could you give me back Your joy again so that I can move on in my life?"

Again, Marilyn and I set another time to go shopping together. When I arrived at her house she said to me, "Thank you Akemi. You are the angel of light." I smiled at her and sensed that God was smiling at me. We did grocery shopping at Longo's again, but Marilyn started having a severe pain in her right knee and had difficulty walking. We came home, and I carried her groceries and put them into the fridge and pantry.

This was the last time we went shopping together. After that I asked her for her list and did the shopping by myself.

Meanwhile her house was sold and Marilyn bought a condo at the corner of Winston Churchill and Eglinton Avenue. She was very excited to move to the new place where she can dine in the cafeteria.

The last time I did grocery shopping for her, she asked me to come into her living room and gave me a new address and said to me, "You will come and visit me in the new place. Won't you?"

"Of course I will. I look forward to that."

I prayed over her knee and blessed her future in the new place. I came home with joy in my heart knowing that God will take care of her very well. I am looking forward to seeing Marilyn in her new condo one day soon.

Easter lily from Janette

April 8, 2004

The Brand New Elevated Garden

May 15, 2014

In the middle of April, the last bit of snow melted from my backyard, and I saw that some perennials had started coming out. I wanted to go to the backyard through the garage, but I had to take out so many things from the garage. I removed a cart to the backyard and hoses to the front and back, but I could not carry the snow blower to the basement.

At the end of April, I called Gary at his office and asked him to come one day and carry the snow blower to the basement. Then he said, "I will come this Sunday, Akemi. I will move the snow blower to the basement."

"Thank you so much," I said.

Then Gary continued, "And we are going to Home Depot to get wood for your backyard."

"Really?"

"Oh yes. I will come to see you after you come back from church. Okay?"

"Thank you so much. Finally, I am going to have a new garden."

At the end of my backyard my husband Ken had built an elevated garden with wood, and he had planted vegetables, like zucchini, snow peas, and green onions. But after he died I had changed to flowers, because I could not eat so many zucchinis at once. It was a beautiful elevated garden. I planted many flowers and enjoyed them. But in the last few years the elevated garden had started deteriorating a little by little. The wood was rotten and the garden was uneven. It was so sad to see the process of ruining of the garden.

A few years ago, I had asked Gary if he could fix it for me, but he said it was impossible to fix it because all the wood was deteriorating. He said, "When it's gone I will build a new one. I can't fix it."

For the last couple of years it was so bad. The soil started leaking from the garden. I wanted to ask Gary to build a new one so badly, but I could not. Gary had back pain and had a bad cold last spring. I just knew that God was telling me that it wasn't the time to build a new garden. I was so sad to see the broken garden for another year. I asked God to give me a new garden on His best timing and decided to wait.

But the elevated garden was so bad last summer that I asked Gary, "Gary, could you call Jerry to fix my garden. I would like to know how much he charges. Could you?" Jerry had fixed my front fence and deck a couple of years ago. He did a good job, and I wanted Jerry to fix my backyard too. Gary said, "Sure I can ask him."

"If it's too expensive I don't have to do it, but I just want to know his estimate."

"Yeah, we can do that." But Gary never called Jerry, so I knew it wasn't God's will. I had to wait for a long time.

When I heard from Gary that he was really going to build a new garden in my backyard, I was so happy! Finally, I was going to have a new garden in my backyard. I said many times in my heart thank you, thank you, thank you.

On the 4th of May, Gary came and measured the width of my backyard, and we went to Home Depot. Gary looked around at the wood samples and ordered 14 planks of 6x6x8 feet. He asked them to deliver the wood to my house on the 9th of May. The wood looked very heavy.

On the 9th of May, a delivery man from Home Depot came with a small delivery car and put 14 pieces of the timber on the front lawn. He must have parked his truck somewhere else because our street was under heavy construction. I called Gary and informed him that the material had arrived. He said, "I will come tomorrow morning and move the wood from the grass to the garage. I will see you tomorrow."

The following morning, I parked my car on the street and emptied the garage. Gary came after 10 am and moved the 6x6 wood one by one on his shoulder into the garage. It looked so heavy. I prayed for God's protection over Gary. After he moved 14 pieces of wood he went to Home Depot to buy material to build the garden elevation. Soon he came back with long nails, long metal sticks, etc. He brought his tools into the garage and started building the elevated garden with the thick 6x6 wood using a level all the time. He worked very hard and by 5 o'clock he put three layers of wood on the ground. He said he would continue to work on Sunday and wanted to clean the garage. I said that I could park my car on the driveway for one night, and he left.

On Sunday, when I came home from church Gary was already working in the backyard and had almost completed the beautiful elevated garden. On the edge of both sides he put one more 6x6 and made an elegant garden. I added five bags of soil to the garden. It looked so clean and beautiful. I was so happy about the new garden! That Sunday was Mother's Day. Gary completed it on Mother's Day. I was so blessed by that! Gary cleaned the garage and put all his tools into his car's trunk and left.

A few days later I went to Loblaws and bought three healthy rhododendrons and planted one in the centre and one at the right and one at the left, and planted bleeding hearts and hostas in between. In a couple of days, the rhododendrons started opening. They were all pink. I expected different colours, so I went to Terra this time and bought two pale pink rhododendrons and planted them in between the pink ones. The elevated garden looked so beautiful!

Until last year the elevated garden was the ugliest part of my garden, but it became the most beautiful part of the garden. It has become the focal point of my garden now.

I thanked God for the new garden and thanked Gary who made the beautiful garden for me. I don't know what is waiting for me this year, but I am so excited about living in the year 2014.

Attacked by Bees

June 30, 2014

I finished the water colour course on the 16th of June which I enjoyed very much, but I had to drive to the class every Monday afternoon. The 23rd of June was the first Monday I could stay home and relax.

My good friend Janette wanted to visit at 11 to pray with me. That was the only plan for that day. By 10 o'clock in the morning I finished watering the garden in the front and back. I had one hour before Janette's visit. I decided to trim the bridal wreath at both sides of my garden. The bridal wreath finished blooming and grew so wildly. I started trimming the left side of the hedge. I chopped and chopped the branches with the garden scissors and finished trimming in half an hour. I picked up all the branches and put them into a yard waste bag. The bag was full. I decided to do the same for the right side of the hedge. I worked very hard to finish in 30 minutes. When I trimmed about a half of the length suddenly bees attacked me. So many bees swarmed around me, over my head, shoulders, and back. I brushed off the bees frantically with the branches I held in my left hand. I did not have any idea how many bees were attacking me, but they did not go away easily. I brushed off the bees continually.

It took a long time, and eventually they left one by one. I ran to the garage and took out a can of insect killer and sprayed it over the bridal wreath. I sprayed for quite a long time, and all the bees disappeared from the branches. Then I found a big round bee hive on a branch. The round gray hive was hanging down from one thin branch, and just one bee was still attached to the hive. This hive was perfectly round and the diameter was almost 10 cms. It was a big hive. I removed the hive from the branch and threw it down on the ground and stepped on it with my boot. Some white stuff came out from the hive and one dead bee was in it.

I continued to trim the hedge and finished it very quickly. I gathered the branches and put them into another yard waste bag. I had cleaned the garden neatly by 11 o'clock.

Janette came, and we relaxed in the garden for a while and we prayed for her sister in Malaysia. Janette dug some plants from my garden and took them home. I had a good morning!

Since then I have remembered this incident of the bee attack often. I do not know why I remember it so often, but I sensed that God was telling me something from the bee attack. I went through this accident in my mind again. The bees attacked me and I fought back. There were so many bees all over me, but none of them actually stung me. It was truly a miracle! I knew God protected me. I said to God, "God thank you. You really protected me. So many bees attacked me, yet I was totally safe."

Then more thoughts came to my mind that the enemy's attack is real, but no matter how strong the enemy is my God is stronger than them, and the victory belongs to me because God is with me. While I was thinking about the enemy's attack, suddenly I remembered the Bible verse in Luke 10:18-19:

"He replied, "I saw Satan fall like lightning from heaven. I have given you authority to trample on snakes and scorpions and to overcome all the power of the enemy, nothing will harm you."

Jesus was speaking to His disciples after they came back from visiting the villages. I really thanked God for this thought He gave me. I said to myself repeatedly, "Nothing will harm me because God is with me," and thanked God that I belong to Him.

The next Monday on the 3rd of June, was a very hot and humid day. I decided to do grocery shopping before it became too hot.

I went to Loblaws to buy a can of soy sauce, but could not find it, so I drove to Longo's. At Longo's, I picked up a few things and also found a bottle of soy sauce. I finished shopping, but I wanted to look around a little longer. Then I saw Carol Hay in the store. We said "Hi" to each other and talked a little. Then she said to me, "Akemi pray for my heart. I have a problem with my heart." She told me that she had heart pain three years ago and it went away miraculously, but it had come back again.

I prayed a simple prayer in the store putting my right hand over her back, and blessed her heart and her good life with God.

We said goodbye, and she continued shopping, and I came home.

In only two hours Carol called me. When I saw her name on my phone I wondered what had happened to her. Then she said, "Akemi, this is Carol."

"Yes Carol. What happened?"

"I just want to say thank you to you. My heart is much better now. Even when I left Longo's I felt the difference with my heart. Thank you so much. That's all I wanted to say."

"That's very nice of you. God is good, isn't He? I am so glad. Thank you for telling me. Have a wonderful day."

"Bye!"

I truly thanked God for giving us victory over the enemy. He is good and He is strong, and we are His. I remembered the bee attack again and smiled by myself.

My Japanese Books were Published

July 15, 2014

Since I gave Mrs. Katsuko Kiso permission to translate my book into Japanese, I received a few letters from Pastor Tanigawa of Mihara Lutheran Church in Japan. In the first letter, he asked me to send him two more books, because he had to translate my book in a short time and he needed a helper. He also wrote that my Japanese books had to be published by the 29th of June, so he did not have enough time to send me his translation to be checked by me. I wrote him a letter and wrote that I trusted his translation completely because I know his Japanese is better than mine. I just wrote a few of my friends' names in Japanese and sent it with my two books. I just prayed to God to help Pastor Tanigawa while he translates my book. It was a big job, and I know that he needed lots of patience and time.

In another letter Pastor Tanigawa wrote me that the church was planning a special Sunday service for the 29th of June, to commemorate Katsuko Kiso's husband's 13th death anniversary. They were inviting Pastor Asami who had baptized me at Mihara Lutheran Church in 1965. Pastor Tanigawa invited me to attend that special Sunday at his church on the 29th of June. He wrote that the church had collected 1000 dollars for my airfare. I was so touched by their kindness, and thought that it would be very nice to visit Japan and attend the church where I became a child of God. But I injured my back a few years ago, and carrying a suitcase was not a good idea.

I called my sister in Japan and talked to her about visiting Japan, but she said it would be very hard for my back with sitting in an airplane for 16 hours, and carrying a heavy suitcase. She also said that by the end of June it would be so hot and humid in Japan, so I decided not to go to Japan. I wrote a letter to Pastor Tanigawa that I would not be able to attend the special Sunday at Mihara Lutheran Church, but if I have a chance to visit Japan in the future I would visit his church.

I received another letter from Pastor Tanigawa. He translated my book up to page 79, and was excited about it. He asked me to write a Japanese foreword and to send a recent photo. He also asked me how many books I wanted to have. He wrote that Mrs. Kiso wanted to pay the cost of 100 books, and the church planned to match it. Altogether 200 books would be published by the 29th of June. He was planning to save more money and print more books.

I wrote a Japanese foreword very quickly and asked him to send me two Japanese books and send one to my sister Sanae in Hiroshima. I sent my letter with my recent photo.

The 29th of June was approaching very quickly. One day Pastor Asami called me from Japan and wanted to see me on the 29th of June. I said to him that I decided not to go because of my back. Then he said that he really wants to see me before he dies. It was very kind of him.

Soon after my sister called me and said, "Do you know there is a big thing going on at the Mihara Lutheran Church? Pastor Tanigawa's wife called me and invited me to attend the church on the 29th of June. She said that Pastor Asami is coming. I said to her unfortunately I can't make it. Then Pastor Tanigawa asked me about you and he really wanted to see you."

On the night of 28th of June, I was excited about what was happening at the Mihara Lutheran Church. Pastor Asami was there, and also the commemoration of Mr. Kiso's death anniversary. Also they were giving a copy of my book to everyone who attended the church as a gift. I could not attend the church but I was so thrilled and thanked God for what He was doing. I truly desire that the Japanese people will come to know God's deep love for them.

After a couple of weeks, I received a parcel from Japan. Inside the parcel were two of my Japanese books, Pastor Tanigawa's letter, and a few photos from the 29th of June. I took my Japanese books in my hands and could not believe my books were published in Japanese. I went out in the garden with my books and sat on the garden chair, and thanked God from the bottom of my heart.

Sitting in a garden chair and surrounded by the beautiful flowers my thought went back to 55 years ago, when I attended a teacher's college in Hiroshima and how I wanted to write a book so badly. I could not fulfill that dream, but God did it for me. Now my books were published in Japanese. I felt so awesome and also thrilled to be living life with God's blessing. I said to God, "Father thank you for what you did for me. You fulfilled my dream in such a strange way. Now I ask You to use my books in Japan to glorify You. May many Japanese people come to know Your deep love for them!"

Japanese translation of Akemi's Journals

Mirabilis in the Elevated Garden

September 5, 2014

Early this spring Gary built a new elevated garden at the end of my backyard. It was a beautiful and well-built elevated garden, and I planted five rhododendrons from a nursery and some other perennials from my garden in it. When the plants started blooming it was truly a gorgeous elevated garden. I thought I planted very nicely, but the left side of the garden was empty. I just left it as it was.

About a month later while I was picking the weeds I found a few strange plants about 10 to 15 cms tall in the empty spot. I had never seen these strange weeds in my garden before and I hesitated to remove them. I thought that I would wait and remove them later. I just wanted to see how they grew and what kind of weeds they were.

I kept on watering and fertilizing them as I did with the other plants, and they grew so big. Many branches came out and formed many leaves. They became almost 50 cms high and 50 cms wide. There were altogether five plants. I enjoyed looking at them as they grew. If they were weeds, they were very good-looking weeds. The green leaves were so beautiful and I started to like seeing them in my elevated garden.

One day in early August I found so many tiny green buds on the plants. I was so glad that I had not removed them, and also I was so curious about what kind of flowers they were, what colour and shape. I saw more than 100 small buds on the plants.

One early morning in the middle of August, I walked to the elevated garden and saw white and pink flowers on the plants. The flowers were about 4 cms in diameter and the shape was exactly the same as a morning-glory. They looked so beautiful! I stood there quite a long time and just looked at them. Many flowers in white and pink were already closing, but what a beautiful sight it was! They were not gorgeous flowers like roses or lilies, but just simple and modest small flowers, and I really liked them. I just knew they were not weeds, because they were too beautiful to be weeds.

One cloudy morning I saw fully bloomed flowers on the plants. Some were pure white, some were pink, and some were pink and white stripe. They were so beautiful, but as soon as the sun rose the flowers closed.

One afternoon I had some free time, and wanted to do what I really like doing. I cut a piece of that plant with a few coloured flowers, buds and leaves, and wrapped it with a wet paper towel and drove to Terra Green House in Milton. It was a nice drive and there weren't many cars on the street. I arrived there in 15 minutes. I visited the information centre in the store. A couple of ladies in light blue uniforms were in the information centre. When I approached with a plant in a plastic bag a young lady said to me, "May I help you?" I responded with a smile and said, "Hello, I would like to know this plant's name and is it a perennial or an annual." The lady took the shoot from my hand and looked at it. She asked another lady about my plant, then suddenly five ladies gathered around the information centre and discussed the plant.

One woman came to me and said, "This is 6 o'clock."

"What?" I said.

"This is a plant we call 6 o'clock, and it's an annual."

"Thank you."

The lady continued, "They form big black seeds so you can sow them next year."

"Alright. You know the plant is growing in my garden, but I never planted it."

"That's interesting," the lady said. "You are going to see them next year again."

"Thank you so much. Now I know what I have."

The young lady said, "I will write the name of the plant on a piece of paper" and she wrote 6 o'clock on a small piece of yellow paper and gave it to me. I said, "Is 6 o'clock a family of the morning glory?"

"I don't know. I will check it for you." She went to a computer and searched for information about the 6 o'clock plant. She said, "Yes, it is the family of the morning glory. Oh, it's not 6 o'clock. It's 4 o'clock." She changed 6 to 4 on the yellow paper.

I thanked them and looked around the greenhouse. They displayed many fall flowers. There were so many chrysanthemums. The green house was so beautiful but I did not buy any plants this time. I came home with a new discovery about my plants.

Now I knew the name of the plant, so I checked about 4 o'clock in the book of garden guide annuals which Ken left me. I found the real name of 4 o'clock. The name is Mirabilis. It was written… 'A genus of 60 species of tropical plants having tuberous roots. The genus is called mirabilis, meaning 'miraculous' because flowers of several different colours appear on a single plant.'

When I read this article from the book I was totally shocked. I really did not know how the plants started growing in my garden, perhaps carried in by birds or a bag of soil. I did not have any idea about how they came to my garden, but I knew so clearly that God had planted them in His garden.

Late evening or early morning I often walked to the very end of the garden and marvelled at the beauty of the humble flowers. Every time I saw mirabilis or "miraculous," I wondered what God was telling one through these flowers? Is He telling me that some miracle will happen in this garden, or wonderful miracle will happen on our street? Is He telling me that I am living my life with hope and joy which is already a wonderful miracle? I have no idea what God is showing me through the plant "miraculous," but I will wait and see the wonderful miracle of God.

The Gift of Painting

December 20, 2014

It has been more than 10 years since I started painting in water colour. Every year I took an art course for 10 weeks in the spring and 10 weeks in the fall at the Visual Arts Mississauga. I had such joy in painting and could not stop painting. During these years I met nice teachers and also nice classmates. I also learned to paint with the Holy Spirit, and painting became such a precious time with the Lord. I enjoyed it so much with each painting.

First my paintings were like my own children to me so that I could not sell them at all, even if some people wanted to buy them. I felt so guilty in exchanging my children for money.

I framed each painting with a mat and put it into a plastic bag neatly and kept it in two big drawers.

Many of my friends suggested to me to have an art show and sell my paintings, but for some reason I did not want to do it at all. I accumulated many paintings and one day I asked God to do something about my art work. I said to Him, "Lord I would like to glorify You through my paintings. Use them for Your glory. That's all I want, because I have such a good time painting with You. I truly thank You for Your gift of creativity." Nothing happened.

Meanwhile I sold several paintings to my church friends. They asked me so often, and I could not say no anymore. It was so nice to know that somebody wanted to pay money for my art work, but deep in my heart I did not enjoy selling them for money.

About three years ago my family doctor moved far away and I needed a new doctor. Soon I found out that many doctors did not accept new patients. After a lot of prayers and effort, I finally found one doctor very close to my house. When she took me as her patient I was so relieved and thanked God for a new doctor. Soon I found out that this lady doctor, Dr. Surangiwala is a very smart, compassionate doctor and I was very comfortable with her.

A couple of years ago when I was sitting in Dr. Surangiwala's small examining room I looked at the empty walls for a long time. It was a very small room but nothing was on the wall except a few printed notices. I wondered if a picture on the wall would make it more peaceful. That day after Dr. Surangiwala examined me I asked her what I had never asked anybody before. "Dr. Surangiwala, I paint watercolours. If I bring a painting, would you hang it on the wall here?" Then she answered me, "Well, I will have to ask Dr. Zhang, but bring it over anyway. I can hang it in my home."

"All right. That's good," I said.

When I visited Dr. Surangiwala the next time I took my nicely framed painting with me and gave it to her. When she opened the package and saw the magnolia flowers on the canvas she was very happy and said to me, "Thank you so much. I will take it home."

The examining room is still empty, but I was so satisfied and pleased at what I had done. Somebody is enjoying my painting which I painted with the help of the Holy Spirit. I hoped the peace of God would come to her house through the painting.

On the 20th of October this year, Elli invited me and my friends to lunch to celebrate my birthday. Rita, Dianne and I enjoyed a delicious Thanksgiving dinner. Since Dianne's and my birthday are only three days apart we blew out the candles on the cake together. On the way home while Rita was driving, Dianne took out a birthday card from her purse and handed it over to me saying, "Akemi, Happy Birthday. This is for you." I received it with "Thank you." When I opened the card, there was a gift card from Shoppers Drug Mart. I was shocked because I did not expect that at all, and also, I did not prepare anything for Dianne. I said, "Thank you Dianne. You are so kind. I feel so bad because I don't have anything for you." Then Rita said, "Akemi, go home and repent."

"No way. I am not going to repent. I hate repenting" and I added, "Dianne could you visit me one day soon? I will show you my paintings. You choose one and I will frame it for you."

"Oh, that's good!" Dianne said. I was so relieved.

A few days later I invited Dianne for a cup of tea. Before she arrived, I displayed about 10 of my paintings on the living room floor. When she arrived I asked her to choose one. She took time and chose one with white flowers. I framed it in the basement. After we spent time with a cup of tea Dianne left with my watercolour painting. Soon she called me and told me that she had already hung my painting on the wall, and thanked me. I was so glad to hear that, and thanked God that I was able to share my painting with her.

On the 12th of December, four ladies, Janice, Heather, Rita and I gathered at my home to celebrate Janice Orr's birthday. Rita came around 11 and we prepared for our lunch. Janice and Heather arrived a little after 12, and as soon as they got into my house, they looked at my painting of holly, red berries and snow-covered green leaves. Janice and Heather both said, "I would like to have a painting like this. Can you paint one for me?" I said, "No, not the same ones. But if you like my painting I would love to give one to you."

"Really?"

"Yes, of course. I will show you my paintings later and you choose one."

I was so glad that somebody liked my paintings.

We had a wonderful birthday lunch, and while the ladies were talking to each other I went to the small upstairs room where I keep lots of my artwork and displayed about a dozen of my paintings on the floor, and invited the ladies to come and to choose one painting each for themselves. Janice chose sunflowers, and Heather chose apple blossoms on a branch. They were so happy, and I had such joy in my heart to share my artwork with my friends. When Janice saw koi she talked about her pond where wants to have fish, so I gave her one more painting of koi as her birthday gift.

A couple of days later I received a kind card from Janice. After she wrote a greeting for Christmas she added, "I was excited to bring home the two beautiful paintings you blessed me with! I think of the hours, the love and your concentrated effort for each work of art you create, and I feel so blessed to receive such a precious gift. I can't wait to put them in their frames and to hang each of them in a special place."

Heather also called me and told me that she was enjoying the apple blossoms picture.

When I received these responses for my paintings I had a deep joy in my heart and also sensed that God was enjoying it too. I said to God, "Father, finally I found what to do with my artwork. I would like to bless more friends with my paintings. Increase your gift of creativity, and sensitivity over me. Let me paint more beautiful paintings to show Your peace."

Precious Home Group

September 23, 2015

About three years ago our friend Norma Lovett started having a Bible study group in her condo. Elli Murack was a leader and five or six ladies got together every Wednesday afternoon. We read the Bible together and prayed together and encouraged each other. We came to know each other closely and established beautiful friendships. Sometimes Pastor Faustin joined us and taught us, and one time Elli's son, Mark, who is also a Pastor, joined us. Elli is a good leader and she prepared thoroughly for every session.

Sometimes Elli taught us nothing but love for several weeks. We had homework to find "love" in the Bible. We took the topic love seriously. From that I learned so much about "love." I learned that love is not my choice, but it's a command, (John 15: 17) and also I learned that God already poured out His love into our hearts by the Holy Spirit (Roman 5: 5). The most important thing I learned from these weeks was that without love nothing works in the Kingdom of God. I truly enjoyed this small group at Norma's condo.

But everything has a season, a time to start and a time to stop, a time to get together and a time to separate. One lady stopped coming, and another lady got a job so that she could not attend the group any more, and another lady fell and hurt her back. She was hospitalized and was sent to a senior's home from the hospital. Norma, Elli and I were left. Then Norma decided not to have the group at her condo any more. I truly thought that was the time to close the group.

Then one day Elli called me and asked me, "Akemi, this is Elli. As you know Norma decided not to have our Bible study at her place any more. Would you like to come to my house?" I thought a moment about it and did not want to drive that far every Wednesday afternoon. Elli lives near Lakeshore Road, between Winston Churchill and Erin Mills. I really did not want to drive that far, especially in the winter. I said, "Elli I am sorry, but I really don't want to drive that far every week." I really thought that our group had come to an end. Then Elli said without hesitation, "Okay I got you. I will come to you. Is that okay?"

"Of course it's okay." I said. We decided to meet at my house. I really wondered why Elli wanted to continue this group and drive so far just for me.

Elli started visiting me every other Wednesday afternoon, because she wanted to visit Joyce at her senior's home every other Wednesday too. I had a blessed time with Elli.

Elli visited me faithfully, fall, winter, and spring. My garden was cleaned up, and then was covered by snow, and later the new shoots started coming up. We sat in the living room and watched the changes in the garden.

A couple of times I joined Elli to visit Joyce. She was so happy to see us!

In the spring Elli started bringing her friend Freda and our group became three ladies. We enjoyed and encouraged each other. In the summer, my good friend Janette took me out for lunch to celebrate her birthday. While we were talking I mentioned how God blessed me with good friends and meeting together with them regularly. Then one day Janette asked me if she could join our group. I mentioned it to Elli, and we welcomed Janette. Our group became a little bigger.

Soon my good friend Rita said, "I want to join your group Akemi."

"Okay. That's really good," I said with joy. Since Rita is a good prayer warrior and she has helped me so much in my life with her prayers, and especially after my husband's death. I was so excited about having her in our group.

Suddenly our group became bigger in size. Not only in size but also the richness of the group increased. I was so happy to have three friends in my home every other Wednesday afternoon. Elli prepared so faithfully every time and led us wonderfully. We were growing strongly.

We are beautiful daughters of God, and we carry the Spirit of God in us! When we get together in my living room I literally sense the anointing in the living room become stronger. We all enjoy being together with each other and with God. We all have some problems and difficulties, but we all know that we are loved by God deeply and are very thankful for that.

I am so thankful for the way God is using my house in bringing wonderful Christians together. The day we meet in my house I get so busy, cleaning the house, preparing coffee and tea, and little sweets, but when everyone leaves I am so content and happy washing the empty mugs.

Now we are praying for the coming election that God's Will be done, His perfect will be done for the election and for Canada. We are praying "He shall have dominion also from sea to sea" for the wonderful country of Canada.

October Celebrations

October 25, 2015

On the 9th of October my good friend, Rita, called me and asked me, "Akemi, do you have a place to celebrate Thanksgiving? Would you like to come to my place? I cook very simple food." She asked me kindly knowing that I can't eat any spicy food. I said to her, "Thank you so much, but Carol already invited me to her home on Sunday. I will bring my own veggies, and Jeffrey and Susanne will give me a ride." I wanted to celebrate Thanksgiving with Rita so I asked her, "Rita, can you come and spend time with me this evening?"

"Sure I can. I will be there around 7."

A little after 7, Rita visited me. We sat on the sofa in the living room as usual with a cup of tea and cookies. I do not know how many times Rita and I have prayed together in my living room, but I really enjoy praying with her. I feel so comfortable to be with her and with our Lord. We talked a little in the beginning and prayed to God. We just thanked Him for who He is and who we are in Him. God is our loving Father, He loves us so deeply. He gave His son to die for us. We offered our thanks one after another. We kept on thanking Him, and I was so satisfied at what we did. We have problems and difficulties, but I believe that God knows better than we do, so we just thank Him that we can live with a loving Father. We thanked God for a long time and ended our prayers. I was so satisfied at what Rita and I did together in my living room. That was the best Thanksgiving for me. After Rita left I took a bath and went to bed with thanksgiving in my heart.

On the 11th October, I went to church and worshipped God with my brothers and sisters in the Lord. I enjoyed praising God and continued to thank God in my heart.

About 4:30 p.m., Jeffry and Susanne and her mother came to pick me up, and we went to Greaves and Carol Hay's home for

Thanksgiving dinner. All together 12 people gathered, and when we all sat on the chairs each one thanked God for His goodness and started eating a delicious turkey dinner. I enjoyed eating a meal with my friends. They treat me as if I were a part of their family, and I thanked God for that. After I enjoyed Thanksgiving dinner, Jeffry and Susanne drove me home.

I had a wonderful Thanksgiving with Rita one night, and with Carol's family one night. What a blessing I received for Thanksgiving this year! I truly thanked God for that.

On the 14th of October my friend Elli, the leader of our Bible study group, prepared a lunch for Dianne and myself for our birthday. When we arrived at Elli's house Rita and Joyce and her son-in-law were already there. Elli prepared a wonderful lunch for us. A little later Freda joined us, and all together 8 people enjoyed the delicious lunch in Elli's beautiful dining room.

After the lunch, the rain stopped so we all went out for a walk. Joyce joined us pushing her wheelchair and walked around the neighbourhood. It was a little chilly but the air was so fresh and we talked to each other and had a nice walk.

After the walk, we came back to Elli's house and everybody prayed over Dianne and me for our birthday blessings. My friends blessed me with beautiful prayers. I was so blessed as if God Himself were talking to me. God has given me wonderful friends and I am overwhelmed by their deep love for me. What a wonderful birthday I spent at my friend's house. I thanked them from the bottom of my heart and also God too.

Dianne drove me home and soon Gary called me from his office and said, "Hi, Birthday girl, how are you doing?" "I am fine Gary. I have just come home from Elli's house, several friends got together and celebrated my birthday. I am so blessed."

"That's good. I will take you out for a drive on Saturday okay?"

"Thank you so much. I will look forward to that."

That night around 7 o'clock my friend Ingrid called me from

Germany. When I answered the call, she sang "Happy Birthday to you" and said "Happy Birthday, Akemi."

"Thank you so much Ingrid. You always remember my birthday. What time is it now over there?" I asked and she said, "It is 1 o'clock now. I called you many times today, but you were out."

"Yes, I noticed that on my phone. Thank you so much. You are so kind."

Ingrid told me passionately how she is helping two native families in North Dakota by sending goods and also calling them regularly. We had a good talk, and I thanked God for another wonderful friend that I have.

The next Saturday on the 17th of October Gary drove me out to the north and took me to an art gallery. I enjoyed looking at the artwork displayed in many of the rooms. I even talked to one of the artists. I had a great time, and Gary drove me around and showed me beautiful fall scenes of gorgeous red, orange, and yellow leaves. I truly enjoyed driving in the countryside and took a few fall shots with my camera. I thanked Gary for taking time and giving me such joy.

I had a beautiful birthday celebration for a week, and my friends made me so happy. I was so overwhelmed by many of my friends love for me. When I lost my husband 15 years ago I never thought I would be able to survive by myself without a husband and children in a foreign country. I never thought that I would celebrate holidays or my birthday again, but every year God has given me a wonderful Thanksgiving and birthday. It is so blessed to be a part of God's family and surrounded by His people who show me God's love again and again. I am truly blessed and thankful by being a part of His family!

The Healing Meeting at My Home
November 30, 2015

In June of 2014, my nervous system became very sensitive and I had tingling sensations. It first started in my legs and then came to my hands. Even though I was able to do everything I had to do, it was irritating me badly. I asked God for healing and sensed that it would take a long time to be healed, so I waited very patiently. Then last winter I visited my family doctor, Dr. Surangiwala, and told her what I was experiencing. The doctor could not figure out what was going on in my body, and sent me to a neurologist. My friend, Rita, drove me to Brampton. After they tested my nervous system the doctor said that my nervous system was alright. She suggested that I take an MRI test and a blood test. When I came back to my family doctor, we decided to wait for a while.

In the spring, I visited a naturopath doctor, Dr. Faromo, who had fixed my allergy about 10 years ago. She gave me two kinds of liquid medicine to drink. They calmed down my nervous system quite a lot and I was so thankful for that.

This summer the tingling came back again. I was a little better, but I wasn't healed perfectly. Many of my friends prayed over me, and I was deeply touched by that. I decided to visit my family doctor again. When I asked her for help, she immediately made appointments for a blood test and an MRI test. The blood test wasn't so bad, and I am still waiting for the MRI.

While I was going through this difficult time, one day Mike Whate's name came to my mind strongly. Mike was the chief of our healing room, and we prayed together for many people. God healed many people through Mike's prayers. One Sunday right after the Sunday service while we were eating lunch Mike came to me and sat next to me. When I mentioned that my right leg was a half inch shorter than the left one so that I had pain on my right back, right shoulder, and right eye, suddenly Mike put his plate on the chair and came to me and took my right leg and started praying. I did not take it seriously and said something. Then Mike said, "Be quiet Akemi, God is stretching your leg." He prayed continually. Then actually my right leg was stretched a half inch and the pain which I suffered for more than 30 years left me completely. Since then Mike left that church and I have also left. I thought about him and wanted him to pray over me, but I could not call him.

A month later Mike's name came to my mind so strongly again. This time I could not ignore it so I decided to call him. I dialed his number with a prayer in my heart, and he answered my call immediately. He said, "Hello." "Mike, this is Akemi. Do you remember me?" I asked.

"Of course, I remember you. What happened?"

"Mike, I need your prayer. Could you pray for me?" I explained to him my physical condition. I just wanted him to pray over me on the phone. Then he said, "Of course I can pray for you. Could we meet somewhere? I would like to see you."

"Oh, I don't know where to meet. Could you come to my house?"

"Yes, I can. Let me see, I am free on the 27th of October."

So we decided to meet each other on the 27th.

I was so thankful for Mike's kind heart and willingness to come and pray for me.

On the 27th of October, Mike visited me and listened to me about what was happening to my body, and prayed over me with a gentle yet powerful prayer, and suggested that I should pray the prayers in a book he had brought with him. This book was called *Come Up Here* and written by Paul Cox. Mike left the book with me and promised to come and see me again. I asked him to buy the same book for me.

I prayed the prayers which were written in *Come Up Here*. They were good prayers and I enjoyed praying them over myself.

My recovery was slow but I was touched by Mike's kindness and willingness to minister to me. I was so thankful and blessed being a part of the body of Christ. I was encouraged very much.

About three weeks later Mike called me and wanted to visit me again. We set the date for the 17th of November.

Two days before Mike's visit, when I came home from church and was changing my clothes, somebody knocked on the door. When I opened the door, my husband, Ken's good friend, Lou, was standing there, and said, "I am glad you are at home. You are a busy lady. I came here many times but you were always out."

"I am sorry Lou. Probably I was in the backyard and cleaning the garden." Lou gave me an old calendar which had watercolour paintings for each month.

I invited him into my living room and we just talked. Lou looked so skinny and sad. He said he had tumours in his body. I wanted to pray for him so badly. Then suddenly a thought came to me that it would be so nice if Mike prayed for Lou, because Mike was coming in only two days. I told Lou about Mike and I suggested that he let Mike pray for him as Mike is a man of prayer. Then Lou agreed. He said, "That's good. I love that."

"Lou, I will ask Mike to pray for you, so when he comes on Tuesday I will call you to come here."

I remembered old days when Ken was still alive. Ken and Lou went out for lunch often. It has been 15 years already since then. I was so glad Lou visited me at the right time.

On the 17th of November Mike called me from LifeLabs and said he would be late because lots of people were waiting for blood tests. He came to my home close to 12 o'clock. I called Lou to come over, and I asked Mike to pray over me one more time for complete recovery, and he prayed for me.

When Lou came I introduced him to Mike. The two men talked like old friends and Mike prayed over Lou. Lou was deeply touched by Mike's prayer, and said to me, "Thank you Akemi. I will never forget this day."

I was so thankful for the way God arranged a healing meeting at my home. I never thought about putting together Mike and Lou, only God can do these things. When I went to bed that night, I thanked God for His kindness and His healing power, and I remembered that the 17th of November was Ken's and my wedding anniversary. I was so glad that I could help Ken's friend, Lou, on that day, and thanked God for that.

A few weeks later Lou reported to me that he was feeling much better. I am getting better too!

The Unexpected Visitors

December 31, 2015

In the evening of December the 6th, I received an unexpected call from Maria Ibagon. Maria told me that she thought about me often so that is why she decided to call me.

"How are you Akemi? Are you alright? I am really concerned about you," she said.

"Thank you, Maria. This is a wonderful surprise. Actually, I am not good."

I told her that I have been suffering from an over-sensitive nervous system for about one and a half years, and it has been so long that I was getting tired of it. Then immediately she said, "I will visit you and pray for you." Maria and her husband Oscar are involved in inner healing ministry at Catch the Fire Mississauga and they prayed over me before, but I hadn't seen her for more than one year, so I was amazed by her kindness. Maria offered to come and see me the following Sunday after the church service because they were having a Christmas lunch at the church.

In that week Sayomi was visiting me from California and was staying with me. I thought it was wonderful to have Maria and I would ask her to bless Sayomi too.

Around 2:30 on the 13th of December, Oscar, Maria and their two sons, Santiago and Efraim arrived. I had not seen Oscar and their sons for about one and a half years. Santiago and Efraim had grown so much! Santiago is already taller than his father. They gave me a beautiful Christmas card and a gift. We sat on the sofas in my living room. Suddenly I felt warmth in my living room. It was such a blessing to have them. They asked me about my physical situation, so I told them exactly what I was experiencing. I was going to have an MRI in January for my brain, neck and spine. Then Maria said to me that her mother had a similar condition, and doctors could not find the reason. But she was healed by drinking a mixture of aloe, ginger, lemon and honey.

Santiago and Efraim were sitting very quietly. I offered cookies and a drink to them. Maria told Sayomi and me about her son, Santiago's exceptional life. When he was 7, he dreamed that he was living in Japan. He believes that dream was from God, and he is determined to follow God's plan for him. Now he is taking Japanese lessons every Saturday and can read Japanese so well.

Santiago even taught Sayomi and me a Christmas song "I wish you a Merry Christmas" in Japanese which we never heard before. We all sang that song in Japanese together. It was such fun, and Sayomi and I were surprised. I believe that God is sending a wonderful man of God to Japan one day to show His love towards Japanese people, and I thanked God for that.

At the end of our conversation Oscar said to me, "Akemi, you are okay. We will pray for you, but you are okay."

"I know I will be okay. I am just going through a tough time, that's all."

Oscar and Maria prayed over me for God's healing. I was touched deeply by their love and believed that God was speaking and touching me through them. I thanked them and asked them to bless Sayomi too, and they prayed over Sayomi. Sayomi and I were so blessed by their visit. When they were leaving they sang the Japanese song "I wish you a Merry Christmas" again and said, "good bye."

When they left I thought what a wonderful Christmas gift I had received from God! He sent me intercessors to pray for my healing and showed me His unchanging love for the Japanese people.

In the afternoon of the 29th of December, I received another unexpected call from Liliana Carmora. She said, "Akemi, this is Liliana. Are you alright? Is everything okay with you? I think about you often. I think this is from God. Can my husband and I visit you? Is that okay?"

I was shocked by Liliana's call and said, "Thank you Liliana. I am so happy to hear from you. Of course, you and your husband can visit me."

Rodrigo and Liliana are leaders of the Catch the Fire Mississauga, and we prayed together often before. Now they are concerned about and wish to come and see me.

Liliana wanted to visit me the following day at 3:00 pm. She said that her husband was taking a day off now. I thanked her for their kindness in their busy lives. On their day off they wanted to visit me and pray for me. They are exhibiting Jesus' love in action. I was overwhelmed by their warm hearts.

Exactly at 3 o'clock on the 30th of December, Rodrigo and Liliana visited me. They gave me huge hugs and big smiles. When I explained my symptoms, they listened to me. We talked about so many things, and I felt so comfortable and also sensed the anointing in the living room increased. They brought the presence of God and His joy into my home. We had a good time with a cup of tea.

I offered them a house tour from the basement to the second floor where my husband's and my paintings were exhibited. I gave them the tour of our art gallery and they enjoyed it. They prayed over me with powerful prayers, and I was so blessed by that. When they were leaving they both said, "Please call me when you need help" and gave me their phone numbers. I thanked them from the bottom of my heart.

That night I truly thanked God for His kindness in sending two couples to pray over me in this month. I also thanked Oscar and Maria, Rodrigo and Liliana's obedience to God. It has not been an easy year for me. I suffered a lot, but God reminded me that He will never forget me or forsake me. He knows exactly what I am going through now. He sent wonderful men and women of God and encouraged me tremendously.

One day left for this year 2015. I said to God, "Thank you Father, you carried me through this year wonderfully again. I will have a good year in the year 2016. I am so excited to live my life with You. I don't know what kind of wonderful surprise You have for me in the new year. Thank you again!"

Precious Winter Break

February 5, 2016

Last October Gary wanted to take me out for lunch on my birthday, but I could not do that, because I can't eat many things which affect my nervous system, so I told him that I could not go to a restaurant with him. Then he suggested that he would take me out for a drive instead.

One Saturday right after my birthday Gary drove me to an art gallery in Halton Hills, north west of Mississauga, and drove me around the countryside where the trees were covered with beautiful red leaves. Wherever we drove the view was breathtaking, with red and yellow leaves. I took several photos from the inside of Gary's car while he was driving. When I took my camera out Gary slowed his car down and moved to the right side and stopped his car for me. I took a few very nice pictures with faraway red hills, peaceful fields, streets with beautiful fall trees, and running cars in front of us.

During this winter, I painted three watercolour paintings from the photos I took from Gary's drive. They turned out to be nice watercolours and I was glad about it!

One day in January Gary called me from his office and asked me how I was doing. I answered that I was waiting to take three MRI's in the last week of January, on Monday, Wednesday and Friday, for my brain, spine and neck.

Then he said, "Akemi, I would like to take you out for a breakfast one morning."

I said, "Thank you Gary, but as I told you I can't go to a restaurant right now, because I can't eat so many things."

Then he said, "I know what you told me, but I still think you can eat at a restaurant. We will see okay?"

"Okay," I said, because I did not want to argue with him.

Then Gary said, "I will be busy this weekend, but I will call you and let you know. Okay?"

I really thanked him for his kindness in the middle of winter.

This winter is milder with less snow compared to the other winters. On some warm days the snow on the grass melted completely. It is much easier to handle this winter, but it's still the middle of winter, and we would have to wait three more months for spring. I did not know what I could eat at a restaurant, but I was so happy because I had something to do in the middle of winter.

In the afternoon of the 6th of February, Gary called me and told me that he wanted to take me out the following day. I asked him to pick me up after 10, and he agreed. He said, "I will pick you up at 10:30."

"Thank you so much. I look forward to that."

The next morning at 10:30 sharp Gary came to my house. When I went out and said, "Good morning Gary. Thank you so much." He said, "Akemi, have you used that gift card at Bed, Bath & Beyond?"

"No, I haven't." I said.

Gary had given me a gift card from Bed, Bath & Beyond as a Christmas gift, but I hadn't used it yet, because I did not like to drive in winter time. I planned to do it in the spring. Then Gary said, "I will take you to that store after breakfast."

"That's wonderful. Let me take the gift card with me." I went upstairs to get the gift card.

We went to Cora's, a breakfast and lunch restaurant in Meadowvale Town Centre. There were so many people eating in the restaurant. When we took out seats I really wondered if I could find anything to eat, because every dish would have spice and monosodium glutamate in it. I checked the menu and was totally confused. I did not know what to order. Then Gary said, "Akemi, you can eat eggs, right?"

"Yes I can, without any spice."

"Okay, and you can eat toast, right?"

"Yes, I can."

"Let's order them." When a waitress came he ordered eggs and toast for me. I was able to eat that food at the restaurant and I was very happy about it.

During our breakfast Gary asked me about my physical situation. I explained to him that I had finished taking three MRI tests in the previous week at Credit Valley Hospital, and was waiting to hear the results from my family doctor. I said to him, "Gary, I have a problem with my nervous system, but I don't have to be hospitalized, and I can walk and drive. I can do everything I have to do. I am very thankful for that."

Then Gary said, "Maybe you have to live like that, but Akemi there are lots of people who can't eat many things. Vegetarians don't eat meat, but they go to restaurants, so don't worry. You can make it."

"Thank you so much," I said.

We had a good breakfast at the Cora's restaurant, and Gary drove me to Bed, Bath & Beyond. I picked up a light blue bath towel and a hand towel, and we came back to my home. I said, "Gary, thank you so much. I had a good breakfast and enjoyed some good shopping. Could you come into my house? I would like to show you something."

"Of course," he said.

When he sat on the sofa in the living room, I showed him three paintings from the fall drive in the countryside and five bird paintings. The last Christmas Gary had given me two Christmas cards. One was written with a Christmas greeting and the other one was blank. He said to me "Akemi, this card is for you to paint," with a red cardinal sitting on the snow-covered leaves. I painted the red cardinal and enjoyed it so much that I painted four more different birds on small papers as cards. Gary looked at them and enjoyed them very much.

I asked him to come to the basement and showed him a painting hanging on the wall. Two years ago, he gave me a special frame like a little door, and I painted a rainy street scene with tall buildings on both sides and people walking with umbrellas. Gary liked it very much. The frame wasn't completed, the backing was missing. Then Gary looked around the basement and found a piece of board, and cut it into the right size and nailed it on the back side of the frame. "Let's bring it upstairs," he said, and carried it to the first floor. We tried many places and decided to put it on the kitchen wall. I removed the old painting from that wall, and Gary hung the new rainy street on it.

"This fits here perfectly. It's nice. Akemi, do you like it?" Gary asked.

"Yes I do. Thank you so much." I said.

Gary did so many things in that morning and left. I really thanked him for his kindness for taking me out to a restaurant and for the shopping, also he completed my art frame. I thanked Gary and God for giving me a precious winter break in the middle of the winter of 2016.

Use My House for Your Glory

March 2, 2016

One day in January while I was in the living room, I started thanking God for His love, compassion, kindness, goodness, mercy and His wonderful protection. While I was thanking Him, I realized that His presence in the living room increased.

I sat there quietly for a while. Then suddenly a thought came to my mind that it would be so wonderful if God could use this house for His healing. I sat on the floor and prayed to God. "Father could you use this room as a healing room? May people come here and be touched by you and be healed. Father use this room as a healing room." I did not know if that thought came from God or just my desire, but I had to say that. Whenever I had free time I came down to the living room and sat on the sofa and enjoyed a peaceful time with God.

In the morning of February the 15th, while I was sweeping the floor, my good friend Anita called me and asked me if she could come and see me at one o'clock that afternoon. I was free so we decided to have a small home group at one o'clock.

Anita could not come for the last two weeks. I finished sweeping the floor and prepared for Anita's visit. Anita and I have been meeting together at my home for several years. We talk, pray, read the Bible, but our main purpose is to thank God, and we both really enjoyed thanking God week after week, month after month and year after year.

At one o'clock sharp Anita arrived with a big avocado and said, "This is for you, Akemi. It's already ripe so eat it soon." I thanked her for her kindness.

As usual we sat on the sofas in the living room and talked, prayed, and thanked God a lot. When our thanksgiving went up to our Father like incense, I felt such peace in my heart and even sensed that God was smiling over us. We soaked in the peace which came from our Heavenly Father. Anita and I both have problems and difficulties in our lives but when we experience God's incredible love for us, our problems become smaller and smaller. We truly enjoyed our blessed time together.

We read Ephesians chapter 2 and 3 and were blessed by His rich words and then we prayed for each other. Anita prayed for my highly sensitive nervous system, and I prayed for her right knee. While I was holding her right knee with my left hand, power went through my body again and again. I just kept on holding her knee.

Anita said, "Akemi, I started feeling heat from your hand. My knee is hot. Thank you Lord!" My left hand wasn't hot at all. I thought that was very strange but God can use anything. I was so pleased to know that.

Then Anita said, "He said, 'Healing is in this room. Receive it.'"

I was so excited to hear that, and prayed in my heart "Lord increase Your healing in this room, and use it for Your glory." We had a wonderful small home group and Anita left.

On the 25th of February, my good friend Rita took me to Catch the Fire Toronto where people gathered and worshipped and prayed to God for the second revival. I was so happy to join the worship knowing when the second revival will come, it doesn't stay in Toronto alone. It will go all over the world and Japan is included. I was so happy to worship and pray for that!

After the worship, we were blessed by the pastors. Pastor John Bootoma prayed over me with an encouraging prayer. When I was still standing, his wife Pastor Patricia Bootoma walked over to stand beside me. She stopped and came to me, and said. "God is using your house for His glory. Bless you," and she prayed for me. I was truly impressed by her words because she does not know me at all. She said that she saw a picture of my house. I had a blessed time at CTF Toronto, and Rita drove me home.

That night I suddenly remembered what I did 15 years ago. Right after my husband Ken's death, I cut seven white Japanese paper doves and attached them to the living room wall, as a symbol of the Holy Spirit. I had said to God. "Father, this house is Your house.

Please use it for Your glory." That was a little over 15 years ago. The paper doves are not pure white any more. Their colour faded and became off-white, but they are still flying on my living room wall.

I totally forgot about that prayer, but God is so faithful. He is using my house for His glory. I have two meetings in my house now. Every other Tuesday morning Anita comes and we thank God a lot, and every other Wednesday afternoon four or five ladies meet at my house and Elli Murack leads the group. We are growing stronger and healthier. I am so thankful for that.

Sometimes I forget what I asked God in prayer, but He never forgets them. I was overwhelmed by His faithfulness and kindness. Looking at the seven doves on the wall I thanked God from the bottom of my heart.

Now I have a strong desire that God will continue to use my house for His healing. I have already asked for that. It would be so wonderful if God answered my prayers even more. I have to wait and see. Maybe someday when I totally forget about my request, God will use my house for His healing in a big way. Any way I thank God for His faithfulness. I am so excited to live my life with God!

The Three Kind Men

March 24, 2016

Last summer when Gary finished cutting the grass in my backyard, he mentioned that he and his wife, Sue, were planning to buy a house in Guelph. He said it's quieter and cheaper over there.

When I heard this, I was shocked. In a brief moment, many memories went through my mind very quickly. Gary has helped me for the last 15 years. He cut the grass every year, and built the new fence in the front and back. When I needed to change my roof, he arranged it for me. Even last summer I changed the entrance door, Gary found a contractor and I have a beautiful entrance door now. When I needed any help I just called Gary and I felt so safe.

I said, "So this is it, isn't it? Gary thank you for helping me for the last 15 years."

"No, no, nothing will be changed, Akemi. Nothing will be changed. I will come and help you," Gary said.

"Are you sure Gary? Guelph is far away."

"No, just 45 minutes drive to here, and I also come this way to my office any way. Don't worry okay? I will help you."

He took both my hands and promised to help me while standing in the middle of the backyard. I was shocked. When I heard his promise to help me continually I did not know what to say. I just said, "Thank you." But I was overwhelmed by his kindness and I wanted to cry.

"I will help you Akemi, I promise." He said again. I thanked Gary and God for His wonderful provision.

Meanwhile Gary and Sue found a house in Guelph and bought it. They were able to sell their house very quickly, and on the 20th of March, just one week before Easter they moved to their new home.

In the morning of Easter Sunday, while I was preparing myself to attend church somebody called me. It was a long-distance call. When I answered "Hello," a man said. "How are you?" I said again "Hello," and the man said, "How are you?" again. I wondered who he was. Then I realized it was Gary. He was calling me from his new house in Guelph. He gave me an Easter greeting. He also told me that he was busy fixing the house. He said when he gets his house fixed nicely, he will take me there to show me his new home. I was so excited to hear that and thanked him. I started Easter Day with a very kind call.

In the morning of the 16th of March, my friend, Diego, called me and asked me to shorten his grandson's pants. When I said, "Of course I will shorten his pants Diego. Please bring them over."

Diego said, "Can I come now?"

"Yes, you can."

"Okay I will do that. Akemi, I have something to tell you, but I will tell you when I see you.

When Diego said 'I have something to tell' a thought came to me that Diego and his wife Gina were also moving.

Diego and Gina lived very close to me, and they helped me a lot since I lost my husband. Diego always trimmed the wisteria in my backyard, and helped me to put a new faucet in my bathroom. Since he is a retired plumber he helped me a lot. One fall Diego and Gina both came and helped me to clean the flower garden.

I thought this is beginning of a new season for change.

Diego arrived shortly afterwards with his grandson's new pants. He said his grandson was going to have his First Holy Communion on Easter, and he needed the new pants. Diego's daughter-in-law had already pinned the pants so it was easy. Then Diego said, "Akemi, we bought a condo."

"Congratulations! You know Diego I thought you are moving."

"How did you know? We finally found one which suits us."

"Where are you moving?"

"To Eglinton and Highway 10."

"Oh that far," I said.

"No, no it's not far. I can come here in 15 minutes. You know Akemi, I still keep all my tools, so when you need me just call, then I will come and help you."

"Thank you so much, Diego."

I never expected this kindness. I thanked God in my heart. I sensed warmth in my heart and said to Him, "Thank you, Lord. You are good. You are so good."

I thanked Diego and promised to fix the pants very soon.

The next day Diego came to pick up his grandson's pants, and took a look at my backyard. He said, "Akemi, your backyard will be beautiful again this summer."

"Yes I know. I will have a beautiful summer."

"Akemi, is that Chopin or Liszt?" He listened to the classical music from the radio in my living room.

"I think it's Chopin, but I really don't know," I said. When Diego left I thanked God for His help over my life.

We had such warm days in March as if the new spring was coming soon. I opened the water valve in the basement in order to water the backyard. But when I opened the valve, water gushed down on the basement floor. I closed the valve again and found the telephone number of a plumber who had fixed the kitchen pipe last fall. Then I called Gary to ask for his help. Gary visited me soon and checked the basement and called the plumber, Charlie. Charlie responded immediately and promised to come next Monday at 9.

At 9 o'clock sharp, Charlie came and went to the basement, and started looking for the problem. He said to me, "Can I remove the covering under the water pipe?"

"Of course you can," I said.

My husband Ken had covered the water pipe and air duct with a thin board and painted it with white paint.

Charlie started removing the covering and found a mouse nest and mice droppings. There were lots of them in the old fabric and pink insulation.

"Ah, this is not good. We have to throw away these boards."

He removed everything very quickly. We wore masks and gloves to clean out the space. We opened the small basement window to get fresh air. It was very dirty, but Charlie did a good job and went out for a while. When he came back he brought a new pipe and removed the broken pipe and put a new one on very quickly. When he finished the plumbing, he said to me, "Mrs. Tomoda, do you want to remove the other side of the covering too?" He was talking about the covering under the heating pipe. He was worried if there was mice droppings there too.

"Do you mind doing that? It's not plumbing," I asked.

"No, no I don't mind. If you remove that let me know."

"Thank you so much," I was very pleased.

After I paid Charlie, he went home, but that afternoon I called him and asked him to remove the rest of the covering and he agreed to come on Friday morning.

He came on Friday morning and removed the rest of the covering and cleaned the basement neatly.

While he was finishing his job he said, "Mrs. Tomoda, if you need any help call me. I will come and help you."

"Thank you so much. Is that okay if it's not a plumbing job? Could you still help me?"

"Of course. I will come and help you. I live very close to your house."

"Oh, that's very kind. I am very happy to hear that."

I really thanked Charlie for his kindness.

He added, "You can call me day or night."

That night I truly thanked God for breaking the pipe and removing the dirty mice nests. I also thanked Him for His wonderful provision over me. He sent Gary, Diego and now Charlie. These three men are so strong and kind. I am so safe to live my life alone without a husband and children in a foreign land!

From Demuth

August 24, 2004

The Month of Healing

April 27, 2016

Our church had a revival and healing weekend with Keir and Callie Taylor from South Africa in the evenings of the 7th to the 10th of April. The meetings were held in the evenings, and I did not like to drive my car at night. I was wondering what to do, then my good friends, Jeffry and Susanne Chung, offered me a ride, so that I was able to attend these special meetings.

The meetings were powerful. Mr. and Mrs. Taylor brought God's love and His healing power to us, and I enjoyed very much listening to their teaching.

In the evening of Saturday, the 9th, Mr. Taylor prayed over people for healing anointing so that God can use us for His healing. We went to the front and lined up and quietly waited for the touch of God. When Mr. Taylor touched my head, I fell on the floor. I lay there for a long time and sensed God's power going through my body again and again. I enjoyed the beautiful moment of God's touch and thanked Him in my heart.

After everybody was prayed for we made small groups and prayed for each other. After we blessed each other a young man came to me, and said, "You have a healing anointing. Bless you."

I said, "Thank you. Bless you too." I enjoyed the meeting and thanked God for this special revival and healing conference.

On Sunday morning Mr. Taylor spoke again. After his teaching, he prayed for everybody needing healing. I went to the front again. When Mr. Taylor came to me he said, "What is your problem?"

"I have a hyper-sensitive nervous system. The doctors could not find the reason for it," I said.

"Okay. Healing!" He touched my forehead. As soon as he touched me I fell on the floor. Somebody caught me and let me lie on the floor.

While I was on the floor somebody came to me and touched both my shoulders gently, and started praying with a beautiful prayer. I realized Melanie, an administrator, was praying for me. When she finished her healing prayer over me I tapped her hand that lay over my right shoulder and said, "Thank you so much."

"You're welcome, Akemi. Be healed completely."

That moment the sweetness took over my whole body. I felt so comfortable and warm. I said in my heart, "Oh Lord this is so sweet."

Then He said to me. "Because I touched you through this lady."

Then tears started coming from my eyes. I cried quietly for a while. I felt so good and I could not stop crying. I sobbed and sobbed for a long time. When I received prayers in the past, I fell on the floor many times, but I never cried like this. It was a beautiful and peaceful cry. I cried for a long time. Meanwhile Melanie brought me tissues, and a little later Jeffry brought me more tissues. I wiped my tears gently.

What a moment God gave me! I was shocked. Lying on the floor for a long time many things came to my mind. I thought that God's healing is still available now, because God put His spirit in us. It does not have to be a well-known super Christian or famous speakers to heal people. God can use us through His spirit. The same Spirit who raised Christ from the dead. Many Christian friends prayed over my situation. Every time they touched me Jesus was touching me.

"Thank you, Lord. You touched me and healed me," I said in my heart quietly. I had the most beautiful time lying on the floor.

After a while I was able to get up, so I got up and went back to my chair. I drove home with thanksgiving and awe. What a Sunday service I had attended!

Since then the tingling in my nervous system is getting better gradually and steadily. It has been such a relief, since I have suffered for the last two years. I had tried not to think about it too much and tried to behave like I did not have any problem, but every time I sat I felt irritation on my bottom and every time I walked I felt pins and needles in my thighs. But this problem is now going away steadily. I can sit without irritation now and I can walk without pain in my legs. I am so thankful for that, and kept on saying "Thank you Lord for Your healing."

I will start a new chapter this spring. The perennials have started growing in the garden, and I can look after the garden without the tingling sensations in my body. Last Saturday Gary had already cut the grass for the first time this year. I am so excited to look after the garden this year. I thank God that I will have a wonderful spring and summer this year. I also ask God to use me for His healing. It will be truly exciting year, and I thank God for that.

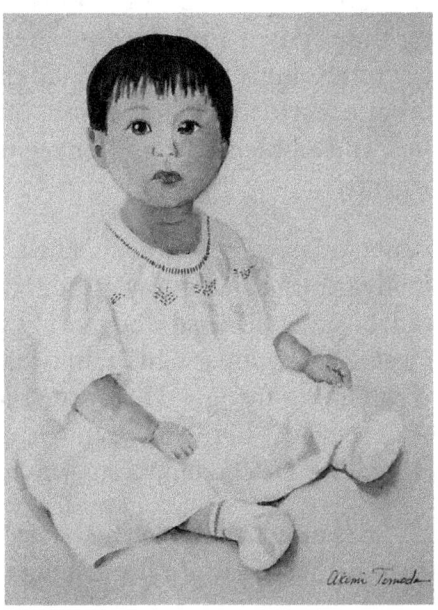

Akemi's sketch of herself as a child

Mike Published His Books

May 15, 2016

One day in early May, when I came home from shopping a message was waiting for me on my answering machine. It was from Mike Whate and he said, "Akemi, this is Mike. I published my books and I would like to deliver one to you. Call me," and he added, "and your name is mentioned in my book."

I called him soon and congratulated him. He wanted to know when would be a good time for him to visit. I said, "Monday is not good. I have an art class to attend and Tuesday morning is not good because Anita Khan is coming here."

"Monday is not good for me either. I will call you and we will decide okay?"

"Yes, it's good. See you soon."

Mike's book was published. I was so excited about it and thanked God for what He did for Mike.

I met Mike at Catch the Fire Mississauga. He was a leader of the healing room, and he was a good leader, he trained us so wonderfully well. I prayed with him a lot and I learned so much from him. But he left the church, and when I published my book in the year 2012 he wasn't there anymore.

I remember one Sunday Mike visited our church, and after the service I talked to him and mentioned about my book and promised that I would send him one. A week later, Mike called me from his home and mentioned that he received my book. He said "Akemi, I only read chapter one, but you went through so much in your life. I look forward to reading the rest of your book."

I thanked him for his kindness. He was actually reading my book. It was truly an honour for me.

Several weeks later, Mike contacted me and said that he had finished reading my book and wanted to take me out for lunch. One day he came to my house and drove me to a Japanese restaurant at Credit View and Burnhamthorpe. I enjoyed the Japanese food and conversation with Mike. At that time, he brought his own manuscript and gave it to me, and said, "This is my manuscript, could you read it and let me know what you think? I was told that I will publish books so I wrote this, but I could not do anything about it."

I said to him, "Mike if you want to publish your book you must pray to God."

Then he said, "Akemi, I want you to pray for this."

I had a good lunch with Mike, but I came home with a big job, reading his manuscript and asking God to do something about it.

I started reading Mike's manuscript little by little everyday. He wrote about lots of God's healing and Mike's healing ministry but his close relationship with God touched my heart deeply, and I really wanted his book to be published, but I did not know what to do. I kept Mike's manuscript on my desk for about six months.

As Mike asked me, I read it and prayed about it but nothing happened. I put the manuscript on the right side of my desk. Every time I saw it I asked God's blessing over it. I prayed and prayed but nothing happened. It started hurting me and I knew that I had to do something about it.

Finally, I called my publisher, Cheryl Antao-Xavier with a prayer in my heart and I told her about Mike and his desire to publish books. I asked her, "Is it okay if I give him your phone number, and he will contact you. Could you help him?"

Then Cheryl said, "Yes, you can give him my phone number."

I still remembered the big relief I had when I heard that and I called Mike immediately and gave him Cheryl's phone number with a huge thanksgiving in my heart to the Lord. I finished my job. It took so many months, but my burden was lifted. I was so happy and thanked God again and again.

Since then Mike has met Cheryl and also the people from Catch the Fire Books to publish his books. I believe Mike rewrote his manuscript and changed it completely. It needed lots of patience and lots of work, and also lots of meetings, but he completed it.

One day Mike called me and told me that his books will be published by Catch the Fire Books, and will be distributed all over the world. I was so happy to hear that.

On the 11th of May, Mike left a message and asked if he could visit me. When I called him he said that he wanted to come to my home at 11 to 11:30 on the following morning. I was so excited to see his book. On the 12th of May, a little after 11:30 am, Mike knocked on my door. He came with his book *Rise Up, a 40-day journey into the heart of God*. The book is so good. There are 40 chapters and every chapter has a Bible verse and prayer, and also a blank space to write down what a reader hears from God. It is a wonderful book. I was so pleased that God answered my prayer so wonderfully. Mike said that there are already many orders from all over the world for his books. That is so good!

Mike and I talked and prayed together in my living room. Then Mike opened the page of acknowledgements and said, "Akemi, your name is written here." It was truly a wonderful surprise and also an honour to me. I was shocked. We blessed his books and asked God that his books would be read by many people and help deepen their relationship with God. We deeply desire that his book will bring much glory to God.

This experience was truly a wonderful surprise from God. It is so wonderful to live one's life with God!

The Running Water

June 26, 2016

June the 4th was a comfortable day. From early morning, I accomplished many things. I wrote two letters and mailed them, and drove to Sears and did shopping. I came home and swept the whole house and mopped the basement and the kitchen floor. I had so much energy and enjoyed doing many things.

In the evening, I had a nice supper, and when I finished eating I washed the dishes, I put the handle of the faucet down, but it would not go down. Something had stuck there so the water kept on flowing. I tried so many ways to put the handle down but I did not succeed. I did not know why but I could not shut off the faucet.

Water kept on coming, and I was in a panic. "Lord help me. Let me shut off this faucet." I prayed in my heart, and called Charlie, a plumber who had fixed the broken pipe in my basement this spring. That time he kindly said that he would help me with anything at any time. When I dialed his number, after several rings he answered the call. I was so relieved and said, "Hello, Charlie. This is Akemi."

"Who?" Charlie asked me.

"Akemi Tomoda. I live at 6172 Townwood Court. You fixed my water pipe this spring,"

"Oh yes, yes. Now I know."

"Charlie, I can't shut off the kitchen faucet. Water keeps on flowing."

"Oh, I am sorry Mrs. Tomoda, I can't help you. I am in the north now." Then he said, "Can you shut off the valves under the sink. Try to find them and shut them off."

"I will try. Could you hold the line, please?" I tried to shut off the valves under the faucet, but they were too tight and I could not handle it. I came back to the phone and said, "Charlie, I can't. I will find someone to help me. Thank you."

"I am so sorry," Charlie said.

I tried to shut the faucet again but did not succeed. I could not call Gary because he lives far away now.

Then I called Diego and he answered my call immediately and said, "I will come soon okay?" I really appreciated his answer, and tried one more time to shut off the faucet. I did not know why, but this time the faucet closed little by little, and the water almost stopped running.

Diego arrived soon, and closed the valves under the sink and said, "It was very tight, but you can open and close them now." He touched here and there, and the faucet started working again. I could not believe it. I thanked him. Then Diego said, "You're welcome, Akemi. Don't panic alright? This faucet is a good one. You can use it for a long time."

After he left I tried to run the water again, and it was working alright.

I felt such a relief and thanked God for restoring the faucet for me. I went out to the backyard and started watering the plants. It was so peaceful. The perennials were growing healthily. I enjoyed watering the plants. After I watered them thoroughly I shut off the water sprayer but the water sprayer did not stop, the water kept on coming. I closed the water valve immediately, but I was so discouraged about it, "Oh no! Not again." I tried to remove the water sprayer from the water hose and put a new one on that I had bought this spring. While I was removing the water sprayer I touched the screw on the sprayer, and I tightened it little by little, and tried to let the water go. The water ran out nicely and stopped nicely. I fixed the water sprayer by myself. I was so happy, and washed my hands and got into the house, knowing everything was okay now.

The next day, on the Sunday of the 5th of June, I was so thankful that I was able to attend the church service and worship God with my brother and sisters. People gathered in the sanctuary and the worship music started. I joined the singing to worship God. It was so beautiful. While I was singing suddenly a thought came to my mind about yesterday's running water in the kitchen and in the backyard. The water did not shut off, and it kept on running. I said in my mind, "Lord are you telling me something from the running water? Is He telling me about the living water – the Holy Spirit God is pouring out over me must go out. I should not shut it off. It has to go out to soak the land abundantly. Is He telling me that His love, His power must go through me to other people? I said in my heart, "Yes, Lord I would like Your love to go through me, Your power to go through me. I won't shut it off. Lord use me for Your glory."

It was an awesome moment surrounded by worship music.

That week God sent me two of my friends to my house. One lady came on Tuesday, and the other lady came on Thursday. We talked and read the Bible, and I prayed over them. I truly believed that God joined me with His Spirit, and His love and encouragement went through me to my friends. I thanked God for using me like a broken faucet and water sprayer.

Let the water flow!

The Bird's Bath

July 23, 2016

About 13 or 14 years ago Gary gave me a bird bath as a Christmas gift. The following spring, I set the bird's bath in the flower garden. The black metal bird bath looked very nice surrounded by perennials. When I put the bird's bath in the garden the birds started coming immediately. Birds came and drank water and took a bath. I really enjoyed watching them. It was so peaceful to see the perennials bloom gorgeously and many kinds of birds fly to the bird's bath and splash the water all around.

Sometimes cardinals came, male and female, and drank water very elegantly. I enjoyed watching their beautiful colours. Sometimes yellow finches came. Their yellow colour was so distinct in the black bird bath. Sometimes 6 or 7 sparrows were in the bird bath, drinking from the edge and splashing water and moving their wings rapidly. It was truly fun to watch. I even took several photos of them. So many kinds of birds came. The bird bath brought such joy to my garden.

However, I also found that I had to change the water every day. Even when I filled it full in the morning, it became half full by noon, so I added water from time to time. I also found that when a robin bathed, the water became brown and very dirty. I did not know these birds were so dirty. Anyway, I enjoyed the bird bath so much in the flower garden. From spring to fall many different flowers bloomed and changed the colour in the garden, and so many birds flew elegantly over the flowers and landed on the bird bath.

Several years passed and I found that the iron stick which supported the iron container wasn't strong enough. The bird bath tilted so often. Then when my cherry tree died Gary cut it down about 50 cms above the ground and made a deep hole in the tree and moved the bird bath to the right side of my garden. It stayed there for many years, but this spring the trunk of the tree was completely rotten and could not hold the bird bath any more. One day Gary came with a black metal pipe and hammered it into the ground, and put the bird bath on the pipe. It is very sturdy and high.

Also the bird bath started rusting, so every spring I scraped the rust and sprayed it with black paint to welcome the birds.

When many of my friends visit my garden, they enjoy the beautiful flowers, and also the birds flying and drinking the water.

On the 11th of July, Christine and her sister-in-law, Dolly, visited me. They both used to live on our street, but both of them had moved. First Dolly moved to an apartment, and Christine moved to a new house. We used to pray together and encouraged each other, but eventually I did not hear from them anymore. We all have busy lives. I heard that Dolly's family bought a house and her son got married. What blessings God gave them. I really thanked Him for that.

When they arrived they gave me a bouquet of flowers. I was really shocked. While we were sitting in my living room they enjoyed watching the fully bloomed garden. Dolly said repeatedly, "This is so peaceful. Akemi, your house is so peaceful." We enjoyed some summer fruits and cold drinks, and talked a lot. It was so wonderful to see old friends. We opened the Bible and prayed for each other. I really thanked God for joining our little gathering. While we were talking Christine looked at the garden and smiled many times. I thought she was watching the birds bathing. When we blessed one another in prayers Christine prayed, "Thank you Father, the birds have water to drink. You are refreshing the birds through water, and Akemi is doing the same thing. She refreshes her friends when they visit her. Bless her abundantly." I was really shocked to hear that!

We had a good time and after they left I remembered Christine's prayer, and I really liked it. I never thought that I was doing the same thing as the bird bath does, but it sounded so good to me. I want to give fresh water to my friends whoever visit me. I would like to refresh them and wash them clean.

Our journey as a Christian is not a smooth ride, so many mountains and valleys. We need to encourage each other otherwise we get so tired and discouraged and can't finish our course victoriously. I asked God to use me to refresh my friends.

I am very thankful that God is using my house and garden for His children. I have two meetings regularly. My good friend Anita enjoys visiting my house every other Tuesday morning, and Elli and the ladies get together here every other Wednesday afternoon. I wish that we all would be refreshed by the fresh water from God.

On the 21st of July, when I came home from the post office, I found out that Joe Lobo had called me, so I called him back. He wanted to visit me. I invited him to come in the afternoon. He came and we talked and talked. I hadn't seen him for two years but we are good friends. We talked in my living room, and we opened the Bible and prayed. While we were talking Joe said, "Akemi, you taught me the importance of thanksgiving so I thank God."

When I heard that, I thanked God in my heart. "Thank you Lord for using me. Let me refresh my friends with Your living water."

The Dry Summer

August 12, 2016

This summer is so hot and dry! We did not have much rain since May. We received less than half the normal rainfall this summer. The garden is so dry that I have to water it often. The field is not green any more. It had turned to brown. Everyday I went out for a walk I felt so sad to see brown grass and prayed to God. "Father give us rain, give us lots of rain. The field is so dry." But rain did not come. Sometimes just a little rain fell. I had to water the garden fully.

When my good friend, Rita, Adele and I visited Inez in Waterloo in June, Inez said that watering plants was banned in Waterloo, and we saw many flowers dried up in her garden. Then fear took over me. A thought came to my mind immediately. If the city of Mississauga bans watering plants, my garden will not survive. I said in my heart, "Oh Lord, give us rain. Give us rain, lots of rain."

At Inez's beautiful townhouse we ate a nice lunch and had good conversations, but I felt so sad about all the plants and grass in Waterloo.

The land is too dry this summer. I did not know how many times I asked God for rain, but nothing happened. It discouraged me a lot.

A couple of weeks later Gary called me from his house in Guelph and let me know that he would come and cut my grass in a couple of days. I truly thanked him, and asked him, "How are you Gary?"

"Oh I am okay, but my grass is not."

"What happened to your grass?" I asked.

Then he said, "We can't water our grass any more. Watering of plants is banned in Guelph."

"Oh I am sorry. That's awful."

"I know, but what can we do about it."

That information really scared me. If our city bans the watering of grass, I can't do anything about it.

"God help! I would like to keep your garden green. Help us. Lord give us lots of rain." I screamed in my heart. I was scared to read The Mississauga News. I did not want to find out about banning the watering of plants in Mississauga.

Just one summer watering plants was banned in Mississauga after my husband's death. So it's only once in 16 years, but I still remember so clearly how I felt towards the flowers and grass. I really don't want to repeat that awful summer again.

"Lord give us rain. Your land is so dry. Help us. Give us rain." I kept on asking for rain.

The next time I met Gary I told him about my concern about watering the plants. Then he said, "Akemi, give water to the plants until you hear that it's banned. Don't worry about it. Just water them, okay?"

"Thank you, I will."

Only on one Friday, July the 15th, we had a decent rain. It started raining at 4 o'clock in the morning. Lots of rain came down with lightning and thundering. I was so relieved and thanked God most of the day.

But after that rainfall, our dry summer continued. Even when the forecast showed 70% possibility of rain, it did not rain at all. I was so discouraged asking God for rain. Actually, nothing was working. I just thanked God that I was still able to water daily up to now. The uncomfortable feeling was always in my mind hoping I won't hear the news of banning water in Mississauga.

The month of June went, and even July went. I am still able to water the plants and am very thankful for that.

On the 23rd of July, I attended a conference at Catch the Fire Toronto with my friend Dianne. While we were listening to the speaker, Robert Henderson who taught about the court in Heaven, said when we go to court in Heaven, it's very important to repent and forgive and ask God to annul what the enemy holds towards us. When I heard that I immediately thought about this dry weather we were experiencing this summer. We need to confess our sins and forgive whoever did wrong to us. We might need to cleanse the atmosphere and rain will come. I decided to pray for rain with my friends.

In the afternoon of 10th of August, we had a home group at my home. Elli Murack, a leader of the group, and Dianne Schleifer came. Only the three of us ladies gathered on that day, but it was a beautiful meeting. We studied Roman 6. I requested that we pray for rain and they agreed. We asked forgiveness of our sins, in natural and spiritual, and asked to remove this dryness from the land. We called the living water from Heaven to our land.

I was so excited about our prayers, and was waiting to see lots of rain come.

My garden is a small garden, and it's not a big deal even if we don't have enough rain, but farmers are suffering so much. One farmer was talking on T.V. and he said that his chickens don't have enough water to drink, and many farmers are worrying about this year's crops. I really hope that Heaven opens and water comes down soon.

Surrounded by Loving Sisters
September 27, 2016

One Saturday afternoon on September the 24th, I felt a thirst in my throat. I drank a glass of water, but it did not quench the thirst at all. It was so strange. I had never experienced this before. I went upstairs and checked my blood pressure and found out it was 180 over 95. I was shocked, and tried to drink more water. After 30 minutes, I checked my blood pressure again and found out it was 230 over 110. I could not believe it!

I knew I needed professional help so I asked myself where do I go? Shall I go to see my family doctor or go to the emergency? I knew my family doctor, Dr. Surangiwala, was working that day, but I did not feel like driving a car. So I called a taxi and decided to go to the emergency of Credit Valley Hospital. The lady said that a taxi would arrive in 10 minutes.

In 10 minutes, I had to prepare myself. On that weekend my trustee, Gary Brady, was visiting his aunt's cottage, and he wasn't around here. Also, my other trustee, Janis Flowers, was visiting in England. I thought that I had to inform somebody where I was going. Suddenly our home group leader, Elli Murack's name came to my mind. When I dialed her number she immediately answered. I told her that I was visiting the emergency, and my trustees were away. Then Elli said, "Akemi, I will come and meet you at the emergency. To which hospital are you going?"

"Ellie you don't need to come. I just want you to know what I am doing. That's all."

"No, no, I will come. Which hospital? Is that Credit Valley? Akemi let me know."

"Yes, I am going to Credit Valley Hospital." I could not resist any more.

Soon a taxi cab arrived at my driveway and I was taken to the hospital. When I arrived only a few people were in front of me and I saw a nurse soon. When I mentioned the reason that I was there, the nurse took my blood pressure and said "158 over 79, not so bad now. You wait here and they will call you in to register."

While I was sitting on a chair and waiting to register suddenly Elli appeared and sat beside me saying, "I am here Akemi." I was truly shocked by her arrival. She came so fast, I could not believe it.

"Thank you so much, Elli. I really appreciate your kindness."

Ellie and I waited together, and I was able to register and I went to an emergency room where many rooms were divided by drapes for patients. Number 34 was my room. I changed my clothes to hospital clothes and waited for a long time. We talked a lot about what God was doing in our lives. A nurse came and checked my blood pressure again, and this time it was 187 over 90. My blood pressure was going up and down very quickly.

Finally the doctor came and talked to me. He said he wanted to have my blood tested and he would come and see me in one hour. A nurse came and took my blood. Ellie and I moved to a different room and sat on the chairs facing a big T.V. set which was showing the Toronto Blue Jay's baseball. I did not feel anxious or lonely because I was with a wonderful sister in the Lord.

While we were waiting somebody spoke right beside me. "Here I am!" I looked to my left side and saw Rita. I was surprised to see Rita. She came to see me after her work. I said, "How did you know I was here?"

"Dianne told me."

"How did Dianne know? I did not tell her."

"I called her and told her," Ellie said.

I truly thanked Rita for her kindness. I felt so secure and warm surrounded by beautiful daughters of God. I lost my husband 16 years ago, and I don't have children, so I am totally alone, yet God sends me wonderful people in my life continually. I felt such love from God and also from my sisters.

Soon the doctor came back and told me that my blood test was fine. He suggested that I should check my blood pressure three times a day for a week and visit my doctor. I thanked him and Rita drove me home. When I arrived at my home, Rita prayed over me. I was so blessed by that. That night I thanked God that I came home safely and also for His love for me.

The next day on the 25th of September, Dianne called me to check how I was doing, and I truly thanked her for her kindness. I was able to drive to church by myself and was so happy about it. My blood pressure was a little high but I was able to do everything I had to do.

The following day on the 26th of September, Violet Royds called me, and we talked about 30 minutes on the phone. Violet and her husband Richard were our home group leaders about 20 years ago. When they moved to Strongville, Ohio, they invited Ken and me, and we visited them at their home. We had a good time there. They came back to Canada and they live in Oakville now. Violet said that she heard about me from Dianne and called me to know how I was. I was moved by her kindness, and thanked her and also God.

As soon as I finished talking to Violet somebody called me, and it was Sandra Laurence. Sandra and her husband David came to Meadowvale Lutheran Church about 25 years ago, and Ken and I became their friends. We visited their place and they visited our place, but since Ken passed away I never saw them. We just exchanged Christmas cards. So when I heard from Sandra I was surprised.

Sandra said, "Akemi, how are you? Are you alright? I don't know why, but I thought about you so strongly that I called you." We talked a lot, and I enjoyed talking to my old friend. Sandra said, "David wants to visit you. We will let you know, okay?" I thanked her. It was truly amazing to hear from my old friend.

On that afternoon Chintsu Michel visited me. Her husband Lou and she lived on our street about 30 years ago. At that time, she came from Taiwan and could not speak English well, but we became friends. She had lots of problems and I started praying for her, and finally I introduced Jesus to her. She became a Christian. They moved from this street, and we did not see each other for a long time. Chintsu came with gifts, and we spent time together in my living room again. She became a strong spirit-filled Christian, and I was so moved at what God did in her life. She prayed over me. I was so thankful to have a wonderful sister like her.

When my blood pressure suddenly went up, I had to go to Emergency at Credit Valley Hospital, but because of it I experienced so many sisters' kindness. I realized I wasn't totally alone in this country. I am surrounded by kind and warm-hearted people. Two sisters visited me at the emergency unexpectedly, and three sisters called me suddenly, and one sister visited me and prayed over me. God showed me His love and His kindness through His beautiful daughters. I am so thankful for that, and realized how wonderful it is to be a part of God's family.

Special Birthday Gift

November 20, 2016

Our home group leader, Elli, asked me one day in October, "Akemi, your birthday is coming soon. I thought about that, but you don't need any gift do you?"

"No, I don't. I am cleaning up my house, and I already have lots of things."

"I thought so. How about my cooking dinner for you and your friends?"

"Thank you, but I can't eat so many things now. I really don't need it."

"Then I will take you out for a drive. How's that?"

"No thanks, Elli. I really don't need that. I am very content to stay home."

"Okay. Do you still want to visit my son's church?"

"Yes, of course. I would love to do that."

"Then that's the birthday gift for you. I will let you know when we can visit him."

"Alright. That's wonderful! Thank you so much."

Elli invited our friend, Dianne, to come with us too, and decided to visit the Christian Victory Church on the 6th of November.

I was so excited about visiting Christian Victory Church in Peterborough and to meet Elli's son, Pastor Mark Murack again.

Several years ago, I met Pastor Mark at Catch the Fire Mississauga. While we were praying before the service he joined us. He asked me to pray over him. I was so surprised by his request, but prayed for him. I simply blessed him, and asked God to increase His grace over him. After the service, I went to him and thanked him for the wonderful message. Then he said to me, "Akemi, your name is well known in Heaven more than on earth." I was totally freed by his words. I don't have to be recognized by anybody on the earth. My Heavenly Father knows me well. That's more than enough.

Pastor Mark's speech changed me and freed me completely. My life is changed in a wonderful way, so that visiting his church has a very important meaning for me. It takes at least two hours to go to Peterborough, so it's going to be a long drive, and I felt so sorry for Elli, but I was so excited and thought that was the best birthday gift for me, and thanked God for that.

On the 6th of November, Elli came to pick me up at a quarter to 8, and we picked up Dianne, and drove to Peterborough. We were driving east. The sun was bright and it was a beautiful day.

When we arrived at the church I was so happy. The church building is a big and beautiful building and a greeter welcomed us very warmly. It was so wonderful to be welcomed. Then I saw Mark and his wife, Wendy, come to greet us. Mark shook my hand and said, "Welcome to our church. It is an honour to have you. Happy Birthday, Akemi."

I was touched deeply. Many people welcomed us and they were so friendly. I felt so comfortable being there, and thanked God that I was able to visit Mark's church. He talked about the importance of relationship with God. It was a good teaching. After the service two ladies prayed for the healing of my shoulder which I injured this summer. We enjoyed sitting in the beautiful building, and I felt such peace in there.

Soon Elli took us to Swiss Chalet. Elli's grand-daughter, her baby, and her boy friend were already there, and Mark and Wendy joined us. They were so kind to spend more time with me. When Mark sat right in front of me, I said, "It was a wonderful service in the beautiful church. I enjoyed it so much. Thank you. Can I ask you a question later?"

He said, "You can ask me now. It doesn't have to be after lunch."

I asked a very important question to him. I said, "When I lost my husband I had a very hard time. All our dreams were gone and all our hopes were gone. I could not live like that, so I asked God "All our dreams and hopes were shattered in pieces and I can't pick them up any more. It's very hard to live like this," and God said to me. "You don't have to fulfill your dreams any more. You will fulfill my dreams and plans for your life." But He never revealed to me what His dreams and plans were for me. I would like to ask you what do you think God's dreams and plans are for me?"

Mark thought about it for a while and said, "When you live a happy life, that's God's plans and dreams for you."

"Thank you. I am glad I asked you," I said. We had a nice lunch and a good conversation at Swiss Chalet in Peterborough.

After lunch Elli drove Dianne and me home. It took two hours. We were driving towards the west and the sun was so bright in our eyes. Elli spent eight hours in taking us to Peterborough to celebrate my birthday. It was truly an extravagant birthday gift for me, and I was overwhelmed by her kindness. I was so glad that I was able to talk to Mark.

Since God said that I don't have to fulfill my dreams, but rather His dreams and plans for me, I was wondering what was His plan. I published books accidently in 2012, and my books were translated in Japanese and they published my Japanese books in 2014, but I always thought that wasn't all of His plan for me. If I do everything with joy and thanksgiving that could be His plan for me. If I paint watercolours with joy and thanksgiving that is His plan for me. If I write essays about the goodness of God in my life with joy and thanksgiving, it is His plan for me. If I look after His garden and do sewing, and even cooking and cleaning my house that He gave to me with joy and thanksgiving, they are all God's dreams and plans for me.

By living a happy life with God I would like to bring light into the darkness.

What a wonderful and meaningful birthday I celebrated! I thanked God for that.

I Had a Good Year in 2016

December 23, 2016

The year 2016 is going by quickly. We have already had lots of snow in December, and many cold days. We will have a white Christmas this year. When I was sitting on the sofa in the living room by myself, looking at the snow-covered backyard, so many memories went through my mind.

I enjoyed many beautiful flowers this year, and also many meetings were held in my living room. My wonderful sisters in the Lord got together and thanked God and praised God. We studied the Bible seriously and encouraged each other. I had awesome times in my house, and I thanked God for that. God is using my house for His purpose and I am thrilled by that. I live a very simple life as a widow but living a life with God's spirit is exciting. This year in 2016 I experienced two new things in my life of faith.

One was that I went to the court of Heaven with my friend twice. I never even thought about going to the court of Heaven before, so it was new to me.

I learned about the court of Heaven from Robert Henderson in the spring. He came to Catch the Fire Toronto to teach us about the courts of Heaven and our destiny. I learned about how the enemy operates in our lives. He told us that the enemy uses the negative words spoken over us and torments us, so we must go to the court of Heaven and ask God to annul these words over us. I thought it was so interesting and so true. Mr. Robert Henderson also taught us that the enemy is a legalist so we must fight them legally. I was so pleased to know this truth.

In the fall while my good friend Anita and I were having our small home group, we discussed about the court of Heaven and one day we decided to go there.

It was a totally new experience for us, but my spirit was so excited about it. We must enter His gate with thanksgiving and His court with praise. We thanked God and praised Him and asked Him to open the door for us. When we asked that prayer I felt total peace such as I never before experienced. Anita sensed the same thing too. We asked for forgiveness of our sins and we forgave people who spoke negative words over us and our families, and asked God to annul these words. We asked that these words be stricken from the record of the court because they are not in agreement with God's heart towards us. We finished our business in the court and came out of it. I felt something changed in Heaven and truly believed that it will manifest on the earth too.

A few weeks later I went to the court of Heaven again with my friend Rita. We decided to go to the court of Heaven that afternoon. In the morning, I was already excited about going to the court of Heaven with Rita. I said to the Lord, "Oh Lord, I am so excited about going to the court of Heaven again!" Then suddenly He said to me, "Me too!"

When Rita visited in the afternoon, we went to the court of Heaven with thanksgiving and praise again and did the same thing. When we prayed to annul the negative words spoken over us and our family, Rita saw a picture of a liquid eraser coming from Heaven and erasing the negative words quickly. That was so awesome, and she also saw a picture of Jesus sitting beside her and He looked at her and smiled. Rita burst into tears. We had such sacred moments and we both thanked God from the bottom of our hearts.

That was one of my new experiences in this year, and the second one was that God answered my prayers that I had been praying for many years.

More than the last 30 years every morning when I woke up I have prayed for peace for Israel, salvation for Japan and the blessing of God for Canada. Since I live in Canada, as a Christian, I have a strong desire that the Japanese people will come to know their Creator. Every morning I lift up my family's name, friends and neighbours names in my prayers that they be saved and live their lives with the blessings of God. I have kept on doing that for more than 30 years, but nothing happened, nobody was saved, but I just could not stop praying for them, because I really wanted them to know how much they are loved by God, the creator of Heaven and earth.

However, recently something was changed. When I talked to my sister-in-law, Yaye, in Thunder Bay, she was so happy to talk to me. While we were talking suddenly she said, "I thank God every morning and every night."

When I heard that I thanked God in my heart. "Thank you Lord for what you are doing in her life." We had a good conversation and I was so encouraged at what God was doing in Yaye's life. She is already 98 years old, and had moved to a senior's home. I continue to pray that she will come to know God closely.

Exactly one week before Christmas I received a Christmas card from my sister, Sanae, in Japan. When I opened the envelope, I found four photos of Sanae and her husband Shigera. They looked very happy, and she wrote in the card, "Wishing you a Merry Christmas and a healthy new year. I will be praying for your good health." I thanked God. My sister in Japan is praying to God for my health. I was so happy to know that. Finally, my sister realized there is a living God who hears our prayers and she is praying to Him.

After 30 long years, finally I am starting to see the result of my prayers! "Lord save them. Take them into Your family, take them into Your Kingdom. Let them know Your love. Give them true life, give them everlasting life."

I am so encouraged and I will keep on praying the same prayers for the next year, the year of 2017.

The Year 2017 Has Started

January 30, 2017

From before Christmas until after New Year, I did not have any meetings at my home. I was free for almost one month. During this time, I received a beautiful calendar from the Canadian Bible Society. When I opened it, there was a beautiful picture of a sunset and blue mountains for the month of October. Somebody took a photo from the top of a mountain. I saw God's beautiful creation and even sensed that His voice was echoing in the blue mountains.

Suddenly I wanted to paint this picture of beautiful mountains. I really enjoyed painting the gorgeous sunset with many blue mountains in the background and green trees in the foreground. When I paint watercolour at art class I use a hair dryer to dry the paper, but when I paint at home I don't have to use a hair dryer. I can do so many other things while the paper dries up. I can cook or clean the house, and come back to paint. I really enjoyed painting the beautiful blue mountain. When I completed the painting, I cut out a mat and prepared it to frame at any time.

Then I painted another picture from the same calendar. This time it was the northern lights from the month of November. It was captioned Mount Kirkjufell in Iceland. Blue and light green northern lights were displayed in the sky beautifully. I painted this dynamic creation by God in watercolour and I was so pleased.

When I finished the northern light picture I started painting pink tulips. These beautiful blooming pink tulips appeared to be dancing happily in the spring light. I enjoyed every moment as I painted the tulips, and I painted one more of different tulips.

I enjoyed two weeks of winter break with painting and was satisfied with the way I started this year. I thanked God for giving me a gift of creativity. I enjoyed painting scenes of God's beautiful creations.

The second week of January meetings at my house started. Anita came on the 10th of January. Anita's mother and I are almost the same age, so Anita is a very young lady but keeps on coming to my house. From the beginning, we decided to thank God no matter what happened in our lives, because God is bigger than any problems we face on the earth, and we kept on doing that. Often, she encourages me and she prays over me with strong prayers. I love Anita's beautiful heart and her big love for the Lord. We had a good meeting and I thanked God for the first meeting in this year.

The following day, on the 11th of January, we had a Bible study at my house. Ellie, the leader of our group, Dianne, and Janette came. Rita and Freda weren't able to come. We worshipped God with worship music and thanked God. Then we had communion and studied God's words seriously. We prayed and encouraged each other. We had such beautiful harmony and I thanked God for that.

While we were thanking God, I thought that these ladies are a precious gift from God to each other. We go to different churches, only Rita and Janette go to the same church, and we are all from different countries. Ellie is from Germany, Dianne is from the U.S.A., Rita is from Montreal, Canada, Janette is from Malaysia, Freda is from Uganda, and I am from Japan. We all came from different places and are living in Mississauga now. I wonder if it is a coincidence that we meet together at my house or if it is God's plan. If it's God's plan to have us meet together at my house at this time, it's an awesome gift from God.

None of us had a comfortable and easy life, but we all went through very difficult and hard lives, and some are still experiencing difficulties. But because of these hard lives we are growing stronger and trusting God more. Every lady is a strong and mature Christian, and each one gives their life to God completely. I am so blessed to get together with these wonderful Christians. What a wonderful gift God gave to me! I really thanked Him for that.

When we get together everyone brings the Holy Spirit with them, and I sense the presence of God so strongly. When we worship, pray, and thank God, we are experiencing a piece of Heaven here on the earth. I desire that God's love grow in us strongly, so we can practice sharing His love towards the people God sends into our lives.

I started the year 2017 in such a good way. I already painted four paintings, and I enjoyed painting so much as if someone was helping me. I am planning to register for the spring art class at Visual Arts Mississauga this year too, and I will enjoy painting with other artists and also in the warm spring weather.

Our Bible study will continue, and I will enjoy having God's hand-picked wonderful sisters in the Lord in my house every other Wednesday afternoon, and experience a piece of Heaven on the earth now.

I really thanked God for the way I started the year 2017, and I believe He has many more wonderful gifts for us in this year. I don't want to miss any one of them. "Thank you, Father, I can live this year with You again. Your will be done. Your perfect will be done. Thank you."

Thank You for Your Help

February 20, 2017

At the beginning of this winter, I heard from many people that this winter would be a cruel winter with cold weather and lots of snow. I worried about that because I injured my right shoulder last summer, and was seeing a physiotherapist. I worried whether I would be able to clear the driveway this winter or not.

I even talked to Gary about this situation, and he suggested that I ask someone to clean my driveway this winter. I thought about it and had a few people that I could ask, but I never asked anyone to help me this winter except my God.

I said to God, "Father, winter is coming and I heard that this winter we may have lots of snow and very cold temperatures. I wanted to ask someone to help me to clean my driveway this winter but I did not. Could you help me to go through this severe winter?"

When the first snow fell, I was able to use the snow-blower and I cleaned my driveway without much trouble to my shoulder. I even cleaned my neighbour Pat's driveway as well, and thanked God for what I was able to do. When the second snowfall came, there wasn't much snow so that I could not use the snow-blower. I used a shovel, using my left arm mainly and was able to clean my driveway and Pat's driveway too. I really thanked God from the bottom of my heart. "Father thank you, thank you, thank you. I was able to clean the driveway. I am very happy for that."

I kept on visiting the physiotherapist once a week, and sometimes I had pain, but my shoulder was getting better little by little.

We had some cold days and occasional snowfall but it wasn't bad at all. I thought I was able to go through the winter comfortably. Then at the end of January I suddenly had an acute pain in my left knee. One morning when I woke up I could not walk without pain. I limped and visited my family doctor. She sent me to get an x-ray, and told me that I had arthritis. After visiting the x-ray lab, I did some grocery shopping because I was not going out much because of the pain. When I came home I had to lie on the sofa to rest. When my right shoulder was getting better my left knee had an acute pain and I was so discouraged. I asked God for healing and to take care of my driveway. I knew it was going to be a very difficult winter. I just hoped my left knee would be healed soon.

Then the following day on the 31st of January, my good friend Janette and her husband, Ben, visited me unexpectedly. They brought a light bulb for me. A week before when we were having a Bible study the light bulb in the living room stopped working. The ladies helped me to change the light bulbs, but I did not have a proper one, so the light wasn't bright enough. Janette bought a new light bulb and brought it to me. I thought she was so thoughtful. I invited them into my house and showed them my husband's and my paintings from the basement to the second floor. Janette has visited me often, but Ben had never been in my house, so it was a very nice opportunity to get to know each other.

While I was showing them my house art gallery Janette asked me, "What happened to your knee, Akemi. You are limping."

"I know, I have pain in my left knee since yesterday."

"I am sorry, Akemi. We are going to have snow tomorrow. Don't clear your driveway, okay? We will come and clean it for you. It's going to be after 10. Is that okay?"

"Of course, it's okay. Thank you so much. You are so kind," I said.

The following day, the 1st of February, Janette called me in the morning and told me not to clear the driveway. They would be here after 10. A little after 10 o'clock when I looked outside Ben was already cleaning the entrance of my driveway. I came down and opened the door and thanked them. Janette asked me for a shovel and the two of them cleaned my driveway in less than 10 minutes and left. I thanked them and also God. "Oh Father, thank you so much. You sent a beautiful brother and sister to clean my driveway. What a perfect gift you sent me!" I was so blessed to have these beautiful people in my life.

The following day I called Janette to thank her. Then Ben answered my call. I thanked him for his kind help and he said, "You're welcome, Akemi. It was very quick, it took only 10 minutes. You want to talk to Janette?"

"Yes please." I thanked Janette and said, "I don't know how to thank you."

Then she said, "Akemi, you don't have to thank us. God already thanked us. You know my daughter called me last night and said that she got a full-time job now. God is so good!"

On the 6th of February, Janis Flowers called me and wanted to have dinner with me. When she comes she brings her own food, and she eats hers and I eat mine, so it's very simple. I welcomed her request, then she asked me if I needed any groceries. At first, I said I did not need anything, but I decided to ask for some so that I would not have to go out with the pain in my knee. Janis came with a few groceries and refused to take my money. She said, "This is a gift for you." I was really surprised, but thanked her for her kindness.

Janette and Ben helped me one more time on the 10th of February and cleaned my driveway in a short time. Meanwhile my left knee was getting better each day, and when we had a big snowstorm on the 12th of February, I was able to use the snow-blower and cleaned my driveway and Pat's driveway. I was so happy for what I was able to do. God helped me so much this winter and carried me through again in this difficult weather. I thanked God for His help and for sending me kind people in my life.

From the 18th to the 19th, we had very warm and beautiful weather. For these two days, the temperature was over 11° and the snow melted very rapidly. I saw that new green onions were coming out in my vegetable garden. It was just like a taste of new spring. The spring is coming soon. I had a very difficult winter with shoulder pain and knee pain, but I was able to go through it because of God's kind help.

I thanked God again and again. We may have more snow this winter, but certainly the new spring is approaching soon, and I will enjoy the new spring with lots of thanksgiving.

Landscapes in watercolour

www.ingramcontent.com/pod-product-compliance
Lightning Source LLC
Chambersburg PA
CBHW071615080526
44588CB00010B/1145